BACK TO ذات THAT

ASMAA AL KUWARI

Your guide back to YOURSELF

This edition was published by The Dreamwork Collective
The Dreamwork Collective LLC, Dubai, United Arab Emirates
thedreamworkcollective.com

Printed and bound in the United Arab Emirates
by Al Ghurair Printing & Publishing

Cover: Lovely Sunny Day Studio W.L.L
Pages: Kasia Piatek, kasiapiatek.pl
Text © Asmaa Alkuwari

ISBN 978-9948-713-80-7

Approved by National Media Council Dubai, United Arab Emirates
MC-02-01-467908

All rights reserved. No part of this publication may be reproduced, stored, or transmitted in any form or by any means, electronic, mechanical, photocopying, recording, or otherwise, without prior permission of the publishers. The right of Asmaa Alkuwari to be identified as the author of this work has been asserted and protected under the UAE Copyright and Authorship Protection Law No. 7.

BACK TO ذات THAT

ASMAA AL KUWARI

Your guide back to YOURSELF

THE
DREAMWORK
COLLECTIVE

I'd like to dedicate this book to everyone who believed in me and saw the spark within me.

To my second-grade teacher, Ms. Mai, who told me that I was a star, and that was the beginning of the birth of this shining star writing to you today.

To my amazing, supportive family I am forever grateful for: my father, mother, brothers, sister, and their kids. I hope my nieces and nephews are inspired to go after their dreams and achieve whatever they set their mind to, just like I did.

To my amazing friends who have kept being my friends even with all my ups and downs while writing this book! Truly grateful for my support system.

And finally, to all the knockbacks, rejections, comments, and hardships that just made me want to be me even more and continue doing what I do. You've been the fire that lit up this star.

TABLE OF CONTENTS

9   Introduction: a guide for all Arab women
18   The 80/20 theory
21   How to use the book

Part 1: Creating Awareness (80%)

27   CHAPTER 1: Acceptance—The First Step in Your Journey to Your THAT
39   CHAPTER 2: Stop Feeling Guilty for Being Different
49   CHAPTER 3: Breaking Free from the Good Girl Syndrome
56   CHAPTER 4: Don't Let Cultural Traditions Derail You from Religion
61   CHAPTER 5: The Voice Within: Healing Self-Talk and Embracing Self-Love
69   CHAPTER 6: Take Care of Yourself Before You Take Care of Others
77   CHAPTER 7: Embrace the Unknown: Lessons from Life's Unplanned Turns
85   CHAPTER 8: Don't Give Up On Your Dreams: You're Not Born to Be NORMAL!
94   CHAPTER 9: We're All Afraid, but What Are YOU Going to Do About That?
101   CHAPTER 10: Don't Numb Your feelings, Write About Them!

105 **CHAPTER 11:** The Hidden Messages in Life's Moments
111 **CHAPTER 12:** The Foundation for Transforming Your Life: Believing In Yourself

Part 2: Taking Action (20%)

120 **CHAPTER 13:** Stop Complaining About Your Life and Start Doing Something About It!
131 **CHAPTER 14:** I'm So Many Things, Why Do I Need to Choose One?
141 **CHAPTER 15:** Envision It to Achieve It! Vision Boards Really Work!
147 **CHAPTER 16:** Setting Intentions and an Action Plan Is a Game-changer
154 **CHAPTER 17:** Self-Care Strategies for Busy Lives
166 **CHAPTER 18:** Balancing Stability and Passion
176 **CHAPTER 19:** Building a Support Network
183 **CHAPTER 20:** Practicing Self-Kindness
188 **CHAPTER 21:** Daily Practices for Self-Acceptance

203 Recap of Key Messages
208 You're Not Alone Community
212 Acknowledgments
214 About the Author

Introduction:
A guide for all Arab women

To every Arab woman reading this book, know that you are not alone on this journey. We share a rich cultural heritage that shapes our experiences, but we also face unique challenges that require us to be strong, resilient, and true to ourselves. *Back to That* is a guide for you—a reminder that your worth is not defined by how well you fit into societal molds but by how authentically you live your life.

This book is a call to embrace your true self, to break free from the expectations that limit you, and to live a life that is rich with purpose, passion, and fulfillment. Whenever you feel the weight of expectations, the sting of shame, or the pull of self-doubt, come back to these pages. Let them inspire you, comfort you, and guide you back to your THAT, your ذات. More on this shortly.

Have you ever had a moment when you're like, *Wow, now this is interesting... how did I get here?* Well, I've been having a lot of those moments lately. And no, I don't mean showing up in my driveway and not remembering how I got home. I'm talking about realizing that I'm actually *living* the dreams I'd been dreaming for myself for so long—they've gone from being thoughts to being my reality.

I'll always cherish one particular moment: I started writing this book when I had a moment of realization and reflection during a flight back home, *in business class*, enjoying the lemon mint juice provided by Qatar Airways, anchoring in the moment of being able to afford business class after so many years, and just looking forward to going back home after spending this trip doing what I love. It was such an *Aha!* moment for me and I wanted to capture it. I opened my handbag, took my laptop out, opened a new Microsoft document—blank—and the first thing I wrote was "Journey to myself." Just like that, the topic of the book was chosen. I believe it chose me as much as I chose it, just like coaching has chosen me as much as I have chosen it. I'd been trying to write a book before, but the clarity I gained at that moment was like nothing I had experienced before. I guess this is what they call a writer's magic, and this is where it all started!

During that flight I was listening to a song that I fell in love with: "Crooked Tree" by Golden Highway and Molly Tuttle. This was my first time listening to the song, but truly it captivated my attention so much that I paused writing and just listened and reflected on the words. I guess I was meant to listen to that specific song at the moment I took out my laptop to start writing about my journey back to myself, because it resonated so much with me. I realized that the lyrics described exactly who I am and where I am on the journey of my life. I am that crooked tree, the one who doesn't conform to norms or societal expectations, the one who rooted herself and grew in the most beautiful unique way that makes her stand out and be seen, the one who has taken the less travelled road to find herself. The song describes who I have become and where I am right now at this moment in life. I have always asked myself so many questions I found hard to answer, such as why should I conform to the norms society gives me if they mean a less satisfying life than the one I desire? Why is it that I forget about myself and think about everyone else around me, hoping that I will finally feel accepted by others? Why is it that I always find myself dimming my own light just so others around me don't feel threatened or intimidated by me and my potential? My quick answer to all these questions is that I needed to go through all that I went through in order to realize who I am and what I'm capable of. Going back to the song, I would rather be a crooked tree, to be my own version of myself, achieving everything I believe in and set my mind to, and, in return, become an inspiration for others to become crooked trees as well, if that's what it takes for them to get to where they want and to be connected to their true self.

Isn't it so exhausting blaming societal expectations for why we've fallen short? Isn't it so exhausting using our family as the hanger for our own sorrows and the parts of ourselves we don't like, because we don't have the guts to take responsibility for our lives, get to know our true selves, and take action?

Isn't it exhausting when we think we can't do anything with our life, simply because we chose not to?

It definitely was for me! I was exhausted, frustrated, and angry, handcuffed to all the things I thought I couldn't do, holding back who I truly was, belittling myself and my aspirations just to fit in and be accepted by others. When I look back at those handcuffs, I have to be truly honest with myself: The only person who put them around my wrists was me.

It's kind of like the story of the elephant and the rope that an executive director once shared when discussing limiting beliefs in a coach training I led. He said limiting beliefs are like an elephant who was tied down when he was young because he was moving a lot, and the older he got the more he believed that the rope tying him down was the reason he couldn't move. And even though when he grew up the rope was no match for his strength, he'd already created the belief that the rope was holding him back, so he didn't try and pull free, even though he had all the power to do so.

If I hadn't woken up one day and decided that enough was enough, I wouldn't be here writing this book for you. I started believing that I had the power to take off those cuffs, pull away from that rope, and live a free life. I had the power to kick and stomp and show up for myself. I know it's not easy to change and shift a mindset you've lived with your whole life, but it starts by taking the initiative and the responsibility—and, of course, a healthy dose of courage.

Many people believe success is a magic potion that successful people possess. Maybe it's luck, they think, or better circumstances, better society, better this, better that...

Some people want to just keep living with what they already have, and that's okay too—*if* that's truly what you want. But if you're settling for less than you know you deserve, whether in your job, your relationships, your business, or any other area, remember that's your choice too.

I don't like fitting into boxes, which you'll learn more about once you dive into the chapters. I play so many roles, and I can't imagine not being all those things. But what makes me able to do that is taking the lead in my life, reconnecting with myself in many ways. And that's exactly what this book is about. It is a guide that will support you as you take charge, find the courage

> **The truth is, successful people are just people who've decided that giving up was never an option for them. They've pursued success as if their life depends on it.**

to reconnect, build your true self, and find your way back to your true THAT, your ذات.

THAT is more than just a word. It's a profound concept that encapsulates the essence of this transformative journey. In Arabic, ذات (transliterated as *that*) means "self." This book is about rediscovering your true self—your identity, your passions, your dreams, and your purpose. The constant pull in different directions can make you feel like you're losing touch with who you truly are. This book is designed to help you rediscover and reclaim your true self, your THAT.

Understanding THAT

THAT represents your innermost being—the person you were before the world told you who you should be. It's the authentic YOU that exists beneath the layers of societal expectations, cultural norms, and the responsibilities that come with the different roles you play. Reconnecting with your THAT means peeling back those layers to uncover your true desires, values, and strengths that will become the compass and anchor to whatever you do.

Why THAT Matters

Reclaiming your THAT is essential for living a fulfilling and meaningful life. When you are connected to your true self, you are more aligned with your passions and purpose. This alignment allows you to live authentically, make decisions that resonate with your values, and pursue dreams that genuinely fulfill you.

The Journey to THAT

This book is structured to guide you through a two-part journey. The first part focuses on creating awareness. You'll explore different aspects of your life and mindset that may hold you back from being your true self. These chapters will help you gain a deep understanding of who you are, why you think the way you do, and what changes you need to make to reconnect with your true THAT.

The second part is all about taking action. Awareness is powerful, but it's only the first step. The next step is to implement what you've learned and make tangible changes. The chapters in the second section of the book provide practical strategies, exercises, and tips to help you take back your THAT and start living a life that is true to you.

Ready to Get Back to THAT?

The fact that you are reading this book is the first indication that you are ready to dive into this amazing journey in finding and redefining yourself. Other signs can be feeling frustration at not being able to move forward with your life. Or it can be feeling anger for losing yourself amid all that's going on within your life. It can also be the realization that you are no longer going to wait around for others to fix your life. These are all indications that you are now ready to take your THAT back!

I have gone through my own journey of taking back my THAT. It started when I found myself living to work and not working to live, when I was pulled in so many directions for the sake of others and not myself, when I was doing things I really dislike, and when I was waking up every day wondering when this day would end. Then I lost someone dear to me, which made me question every single thing and whether I was living for a purpose or not. I was lost, afraid, and frustrated, seeing others around me succeed, and feeling jealous because I didn't know what I wanted to be successful at. I had all these dreams, yet I kept postponing them because I didn't feel I deserved to pursue them, that it wasn't the right time to think about ME. This was what was going on until I was introduced to coaching back in 2018. I decided to work with a coach to become a better version of myself and to find answers to all the questions I had, such as

- *Why don't I feel like I deserve to follow my dreams?*
- *What do I really want?*

- *Why don't I feel confident enough to stop others deciding things on my behalf?*
- *What's holding me back from taking charge of my OWN life?*
- *Why do I feel the way I feel about myself?*

I started working with a coach to find answers to those questions and more because I was told that coaching helps you create awareness of yourself and what goes on in your mind, which then will support you to take action toward want you want to achieve and become the best version of yourself.

Let me tell you, those days during coaching training were some of the most emotionally difficult days of my life (I was twenty-eight back then). I was drained every single day for over three months, digging deeper and deeper in understanding myself, my strengths, my weaknesses, my limiting beliefs, my sabotaging cycles and habits. I learnt to let go of everything that wasn't serving me and, most important, how to forgive myself and let go.

That was the beginning of my journey in getting back to THAT, getting back to that girl who was told she was a star when she was in second grade, that girl who wanted to do something for the world, that girl who stopped blaming others and society for her reality and started taking action, that girl who finally said enough is enough and now it's time to show the world who Asmaa really is! Suddenly I had a sense of power and control over myself, and I felt responsible for myself and held myself accountable for my actions. I then wanted to surround myself with people on the same wavelength in order to create that accountability and support, which was when I established the *You're Not Alone* community. It's become a safe space for women to flourish and find their own way back to their THAT, and it's a place where I can share my expertise and experience as a coach. As of September 2024, we have more than one hundred members of this community who hold space for one another and support one another within their own journeys of getting back to their THAT. I am so proud of them all.

Remember, this journey is about you. It's about shedding the layers that no longer serve you and embracing the person you truly are. It's about finding the courage to live authentically and pursue the life you deserve. This book is your guide, but the journey is led by you. Take your time, be patient with yourself, and embrace every step of the way.

So, let's embark on this journey together. It's time to take back your THAT and live the life you've always dreamed of. This is your moment to rediscover, reclaim, and celebrate your true self.

The 80/20 theory

In this book, we explore the journey of rediscovering and reclaiming your true self through the lens of the 80/20 theory. This theory is simple yet profound: 80 percent of the journey is about creating awareness, and 20 percent is about taking action based on that awareness. Let's delve deeper into what this means and how it applies to your journey.

The 80 Percent: Creating Awareness
Awareness is the foundation of transformation. It's about understanding who you are at your core, recognizing the patterns and beliefs that have shaped your life, and identifying what truly matters to you. This process involves deep introspection and reflection. Here's what the awareness part entails:

- **Self-reflection:** taking a closer look at your thoughts, emotions, and behaviors; understanding why you think and act the way you do
- **Identifying patterns:** recognizing recurring themes in your life—both positive and negative—including habits, relationships, and choices that either support or hinder your growth

- **Understanding beliefs**: exploring the beliefs you hold about yourself and the world, and identifying which beliefs empower you and which ones limit you
- **Connecting with your true self:** peeling back the layers of societal expectations and cultural norms to connect with your authentic self—your THAT—and building on that the true image of how you show up for yourself
- **Recognizing your strengths and weaknesses**: being honest about your strengths and areas for improvement and embracing both as integral parts of your journey

This part of the journey is introspective. It requires patience, honesty, and a willingness to face yourself without judgment. You'll be creating a solid foundation of self-awareness upon which you can build a more authentic and fulfilling life.

The 20 Percent: Taking Action

Awareness alone is not enough. It's a powerful starting point, but true transformation happens when you act based on that awareness. The 20 percent of the journey involves these steps:

- **Setting goals:** defining clear, actionable goals that align with your newfound awareness; these goals should be specific, measurable, achievable, relevant, and time-bound (SMART)
- **Developing a plan:** creating a step-by-step plan to achieve your goals, and breaking down larger goals into smaller, manageable tasks.
- **Implementing change/building habits:** taking concrete steps to make changes in your life, which might involve

adopting new habits, altering your daily routine, or making significant life decisions
- **Overcoming obstacles:** recognizing and addressing the challenges that arise along the way, and developing strategies to stay motivated and resilient
- **Reflecting and adjusting:** continuously reflecting on your progress and making necessary adjustments, then celebrating your achievements and learning from setbacks

Taking action requires courage, discipline, and persistence. It's about moving beyond your comfort zone and taking the necessary steps to create the life you desire.

The first part of this book focuses on creating awareness, each chapter addressing a different aspect of your life and mindset with stories and incidences you might find familiar to what you have gone through. The second part provides practical steps and exercises to help you act on the insights you've gained.

Remember, the journey of self-discovery and transformation is ongoing. The 80/20 theory is a guide to help you balance introspection with action. By dedicating time to both, you will be better equipped to reclaim your THAT and live a more empowered and authentic life. Embrace the process, trust yourself, and know that every step brings you closer to the true you.

How to use
the book

This book is designed to be your companion on the transformative journey of rediscovering and reclaiming your true self. Here's how you can get the most out of it.

Read with an open mind and heart. This book is filled with insights, exercises, and reflections that may challenge your current way of thinking. Approach each chapter with an open mind and a willingness to embrace new perspectives. Let go of any preconceived notions and be ready to explore your inner world.

Take your time. There's no rush. Read at your own pace. Some chapters might resonate with you more than others, and that's okay. Spend time on the sections that speak to you and revisit them whenever needed. Allow yourself the space to absorb and reflect on the content deeply.

Engage with the exercises. Throughout the book, you'll find practical exercises, reflection prompts, and worksheets. These are designed to help you put your insights into action. Take the time to complete them thoughtfully. Write down your thoughts, dreams, and plans. These exercises are your tools for self-discovery and growth.

Reflect and journal. Keep a journal handy as you read through the book. Use it to jot down your reflections, insights, and any emotions that come up. Journaling is a powerful way to process your thoughts and track your progress. It can also serve as a valuable record of your journey. If you don't have a reflective journal, you can get a digital reflective journal immediately: Find the link to the journal on my Instagram account @coach_asmaaa.

Be kind to yourself. This journey is about growth, not perfection. Be gentle with yourself as you navigate through the chapters. It's okay to feel challenged, emotional, or even resistant at times. Acknowledge these feelings and allow yourself to move through them with compassion.

Connect with the community. If possible, find a friend or a group to read and discuss the book with. Sharing your journey with others can provide additional insights, support, and motivation. If you're comfortable, join online forums or local groups where you can connect with others on similar paths. Please do join our community, *You're Not Alone*. You can follow us on @yna_community.

Revisit and reflect. *Back to That* is a book you can return to whenever you feel the need. Life is ever-changing, and different chapters might resonate with you at different times. Use this book as a lifelong companion, a source of inspiration, and a guide to help you stay aligned with your true self.

Take action. The final part of the book focuses on practical actions you can take to implement the insights you've gained. Don't skip this part! Taking action is essential to bringing about real change. Use the strategies and tips provided to start making tangible steps toward your goals.

Celebrate your progress. Recognize and celebrate your achievements, no matter how small they may seem. Every step forward is a victory. Reflect on how far you've come and give yourself credit for your efforts.

Remember, this book is for you. It's about your journey, your growth, and your path to reclaiming your true self. Dive in with curiosity and courage, and let *Back to That* be your guide to a more empowered and authentic you.

Happy reading and reclaiming your THAT!

PART 1:
Creating Awareness

Chapter 1:
Acceptance—The First Step in Your Journey to Your THAT

I identify as a Muslim Arab woman with a global mindset. I don't see myself as a typical Arab Muslim woman, nor do I fully align with the label of a global citizen. My life has been a tapestry woven from diverse experiences: My family lived in the United States for about fifteen years, and moving back to Qatar in 1998 was like stepping into a different world. I was nine years old, and the Qatar I knew at that time was not what it is today. My sense of identity, my worldview, and even the way I carried myself had already been shaped by my time in the U.S.

Returning to Qatar was like entering a new dimension, one with different rules, expectations, and cultural norms. What was acceptable before suddenly wasn't. I had to reassess everything, from how I spoke to how I dressed, all to fit into this new society. This kind of cultural shift really messes with your mind and values, making you question who you truly are at the core. I found myself altering my behavior, suppressing my natural instincts, just to be accepted. I felt like an outsider, an alien who didn't quite belong.

This feeling was compounded by the labels we were given. My siblings and I were often referred to as "عيال امريكا" or "the kids of America," whenever we did something that didn't fit the local norms, such as speaking with an American accent or not knowing certain cultural references. My siblings reacted in different ways. Some chose to blend in, dropping their American accents and adopting the local dialect to fit in more seamlessly. I chose to hide. I played small, focusing on people-pleasing, always saying yes and going with the flow, putting on a mask outside but being myself when I was safely back home with my family.

Living a dual life was exhausting. I was one person in public and someone entirely different at home. As I grew older, the weight of this duality became unbearable. The more I tried to conform, the further I drifted from my true self.

Then, one day, I made a decision that would change everything. I chose to take charge of my life and embrace who I really am: a bubbly, adventurous, outspoken woman who enjoys life and who isn't afraid to be different. I stopped hiding behind the expectations of society. I stopped blaming society for the person I had become, because I realized that I had chosen to wear that mask. I had been afraid of rejection, of being different, and of being alone, and because I feared these things, I saw them everywhere, reinforcing my decision to keep hiding.

All that I went through led me to change paths and to become a coach. But before becoming a coach officially, I hired my own coach to support me. The first question she asked me was, "Are you willing to take responsibility for everything that has happened to you?" My first response in my head was *NO*

WAY, because I felt like what I was going through was not my problem but was truly the making of others, or circumstances that got me to where I was at that moment. I didn't reply, but then she asked me again! I got so defensive because I was in a state where I was blaming everything and everyone else. She then asked me the third time, and I angrily said, "Why would I take responsibility for what has happened to me when it wasn't my fault?"

Silence rose at this point. She took a pause then responded in a way that changed my whole outlook on life. She said, "Yes, we do not control what has happened to us, but we do control what we allow to affect us and what we don't, so technically everything that you have built in your head about yourself and the world around you is what you chose to believe. Taking responsibility for that will be the first step toward working on the best version of yourself. I'm not blaming you for what has happened to you, but being accountable to yourself is the first step toward the change you want for you to move forward in your life."

That hit me in my core. I had so many flashbacks to times when it was easier to blame others rather than be accountable to myself. Her words ring in my head to this day, because when you grow up believing that everything around you is forcing you to become something that you're not, you end up becoming a victim. And the solution to that is acceptance.

I asked her what steps I needed to take to accept. Her response was to ask me what I believed I needed to do to feel like I could let go of the past and be present with myself to move forward.

At that moment I chose to
- stop blaming myself for being a people pleaser.
- stop blaming my parents for who they were, because they did what they knew was best and their journey is different than mine.
- stop feeling sorry for myself and belittling myself because of how I compare myself to others.
- stop procrastinating from fear of not doing things perfectly and just start doing them.
- stop putting myself last and start filling my own cup with love and attention.
- stop finding reasons for why I won't make it and start listing reasons for why I can.
- start believing that I deserve a better life.
- start believing that taking care of myself is not selfish.
- start showing up for myself every single day.
- start being grateful for the journey I've been through.
- start adapting a more positive mindset toward myself.

Changing how you perceive yourself is the definition of change, and the way to start doing that is by accepting where you are at this moment and believing one way or another that you are where you need to be, with the awareness you have, with the knowledge you have about yourself, with the strengths you have, and with all the possibilities you have to become better. Accepting where I was led me to let go of what was not serving me and to move toward what would. Accepting was the tough conversation I needed to have with myself in order to move from point A to point B. Accepting myself meant no more excuses. That is the beauty of getting back to your THAT and reclaiming your power. This led me to make some tough decisions, such as letting go of an amazing job (in the eyes of others) in order to pursue my dreams and to take care of my mental health; to start coaching, which was still a new industry in Qatar; to start a new idea of a community people were not used to; to create a business from scratch; and to help hundreds of individuals get back to their THAT and live a life of purpose.

It's easier said than done because a lot of us don't want to accept that the key to change and getting back your THAT is actually within you! You just need to take charge and start.

> **To accept who you are now means to take responsibility for all the actions you took or didn't take, which made you who you are today.**

Women tend to feel there are many things that make us lose control of who we truly are. Some elements in the mix are traditions, culture, community, beliefs, the educational system, the patriarchal society we live in that affects both our personal and professional lives... the list can go on and on. And sometimes we feel like, yes, we do have control but we are tired of fighting against the wave and resisting the expectations of others.

How many times have you questioned your thoughts, ideas, and creativity because the first thing that comes to your mind is *Will I be allowed to do this or say this or do this in such a society or not?*

How many times have you refrained from sharing your true opinions and thoughts because you feared being misunderstood or judged?

How many times have you shared your thoughts and opinions about certain things, for example your aspirations, or even questioned traditions, and all that happened is that it backfired on you, which made things even worse?

I've had many clients who grew up believing that it's inappropriate for women to talk back to others or question sensitive topics such as culture, tradition, or even religion. Many of these women have been dealing with the good girl syndrome that tends to make them believe that it is unacceptable to voice their opinions or protest when their boundaries have been crossed. We will go into more detail about this topic specifically in another chapter. But because of such beliefs, they have lost themselves and their voices, lost their sense of identity, and have become someone they're not.

I agree, it's not easy being a woman and fighting your way through the patriarchal societies we live in. But if we as women don't stand up and be the change we look for, nothing will ever change.

The first thing we need to do is start being accountable to ourselves and our actions.

I remember clearly how all these barriers didn't really matter to me when I was just a little girl. I remember having the freedom to be myself and try, explore and discover what life had to offer. How many of us can say that about her life right now?

But let's just take a moment and change that.

If change doesn't come from within, then things around us won't change either.

Ask yourself these questions:
- When was the last time you did something without first thinking about the consequences?
- When was the last time you were just being you?
- When was the last time you truly had fun?
- When was the last time you laughed so hard you got stomach cramps?
- When was the last time you did something just for you?

If you answered "quite a long time ago" to most of the questions, then you are exactly where you need to be.

And if you answered "very recently" to most of the questions, then you are exactly where you need to be as well.

This book is not a one-mold-fits-all. This book is here to support you in finding yourself, getting to know yourself all over again, and, most important, finding your way back to your THAT.

It is your journey that you take in this world. Each one of us has their own. No matter how similar or different our backgrounds are, even if we were brought up in the same house and with the same parents, each of us experiences life differently and has different versions of our parents. Yes, we have gone through so much, no one can deny us our experiences and our emotions because it was we who went through it and nobody else. So, take the time to acknowledge what you went through and how you felt during each stage of your life (if you need to, pause for a moment here and reflect).

But for you to take responsibility now, you need to accept where you are.

You might have imagined your life slightly differently at this point of time. I had imagined that I would be married with three kids, be a working mom with an amazing job, and have my own business. Well, I can tell you that my life turned out a bit differently. I am a thirty-five-year-young woman, single, have two businesses and an amazing job, and I am the happiest I have been, *elhamdullah*. Was it exactly how I imagined my life to be? Not really, but it's very close. And the most important thing to admit is that God has chosen the best path for me at this moment. I truly believe that with all my heart. I always say that I don't know if I would be who I am today had I got what I specifically wished for, and that's because Allah knows what's best for us. Everything comes at the right time when we are truly ready for it.

This is now the right time for me to be where I am, and I'm certain that it is the right time for you to be where you are as well. It's not because you don't deserve the best. Sometimes we need to go through certain situations to know ourselves, to know how strong we are, or how much we need to grow to be ready for what we have asked for. We need to have a change of perspective and understand our worth, and most importantly, we need to find ourselves again amidst all that has happened to us.

Accepting where you are now is what you need to do to be able to move forward. Holding a grudge toward life will never allow you to flip the page and start writing your journey toward a better life. Accepting means that I know my strengths as well as my weaknesses. Accepting means learning about what I know and what I may not know (my blind spots). Accepting is taking responsibility for my actions up to this point and being aware of all the actions I will take in the future. Accepting is learning to understand what's serving you and what's not.

Everything in life is a choice, and whether we choose or don't is also our choice.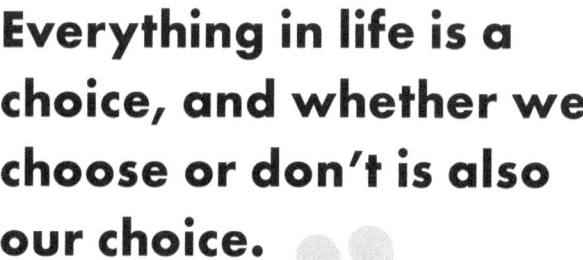

This fundamental truth is what sets us apart from every other living being on this planet. God created us with the unique ability to choose who we are, what we believe in, whether to do right or wrong, how we live our lives, and even how we react to the world around us. Every single day, every single moment, we are faced with choices that shape the course of our lives.

We choose how to spend our time, what goals we pursue, where we want to go, who we love, and how we express that love. Even when it feels as though so much is beyond our control—our family, our upbringing, the circumstances we're born into—the power to choose how we respond to those circumstances is always within our hands.

When you consider all the factors that have shaped your life so far—your parents, your cultural background, the country you were born in, even the language you speak—it's easy to think, *I didn't choose any of this.* And that's true. These elements were handed to you without your input, forming the backdrop of your life. But how you interact with these factors, how you let them influence you, and how you decide to shape your life moving forward *are* all within your control, hence the power of acceptance at the beginning of your journey.

Taking responsibility for my choices, recognizing that I had allowed others to dictate who I was, was one of the hardest things I've ever worked on. But it was also the most liberating. It was essential for me to become the person I am today and to accept where I was at that moment.

I've had clients come to me saying they want to change. They want to be more confident, happier, more content. The first thing I ask them is, *"Are you willing to take responsibility for every action and reaction you've had up to this point?"* If their answer is yes, I know I can help them achieve their goals. But if they're not ready to accept that responsibility, then they're not ready to change. Because if you can't own up to your own life, you'll always blame something or someone else for where you are.

Your life is your choice. Not choosing is still a choice, and once you understand that, once you fully grasp the responsibility you have toward yourself, you'll realize just how much power you have to shape your destiny. This realization is the biggest game-changer you will ever experience.

In life, every decision we make, whether consciously or subconsciously, shapes our path and influences our future. Conscious choices align with our values and goals, guiding us toward a life of purpose and fulfillment. They empower us to live intentionally, ensuring that our actions reflect who we truly are. On the other hand, subconscious choices often lead us astray, driven by impulses, societal pressures, or unexamined motivations. These choices can result in outcomes that do not serve our best interests, leading to regret and a sense of powerlessness.

As Muslims, we understand that although we have the power of choice, it is intricately woven with our faith in *qadr*—the divine decree. Islam teaches us that although fate is preordained by Allah, we are given the free will to make choices within that framework. Every choice we make is an exercise of that free will, but it is also a manifestation of faith, trusting that Allah's plan is always unfolding, even when the outcome is beyond our control. Faith allows us to see that our choices are a form of responsibility, and at the same time, a surrender to the greater wisdom of the Almighty.

This delicate balance of faith and fate encourages us to be mindful in our decisions, recognizing that though we hold the reins, Allah's guidance is ever-present, shaping outcomes we may not always foresee. By making conscious choices aligned with our faith and values, we are actively participating in shaping our destiny, knowing that whatever happens, it is for our ultimate good.

Remember, your life is your choice. Every moment, every action, every reaction is within your control, and yet, it is also a testament to your faith in Allah's plan. It's time to embrace that power—rooted in both faith and free will—and start making choices that reflect the life you truly want to live, all while trusting in the divine wisdom that guides you forward.

Chapter 2:
Stop Feeling Guilty for Being Different

Growing up, one of the many beliefs I had engraved in me was that being different was somehow wrong. The message was loud and clear: Thinking differently, acting differently, or simply being different was something to be avoided. This idea was deeply rooted in the belief that society functions best when everyone is the same, when everyone is "normal." But what is normal, really? Who decides what it means to be normal?

In collectivist societies such as ours, the pressure to conform and not be different can be overwhelming. There is an unspoken understanding that to belong, you must fit a certain mold. But as I've come to realize over the years, normalcy is not as clear-cut as it seems. The word "normal" is linked to the concept of "norms," which are behaviors that have become familiar through repetition. If we think about it, what we consider normal today might have once been a unique, even strange behavior. Over time, as more people adopted this behavior, it became the norm. This raises the question: Is anything truly normal? Or is everything we see as normal just a collection of once-unique behaviors that have been repeated often enough to become accepted?

Theoretically, none of us are born with a set understanding of what is normal. We enter the world as blank slates, free from preconceived notions of how we should think, act, or be. As we grow, our perceptions are shaped by our families, the religions we're born into, our cultures, traditions, traumas, and other life experiences. These influences create the person we become, but they also place restrictions on how far we can stray from the pre-defined boxes that society expects us to fill. We are encouraged to follow the road most traveled, to fit into ready-made molds that have been passed down through generations, and to ignore the road less traveled, even though that road might suit you better.

Some might argue that there are advantages to being normal. It's easier, they say, because the path has already been paved by those who came before us. By staying within the boundaries, we can avoid danger, uncertainty, and backlashes. Others might say that normalcy provides a sense of belonging; that by fitting in, we understand ourselves better because we are not alone. There's also the comfort of being part of a group, whether it's a family, society, or generation, and as humans that creates a sort of comfort for us as well.

But what would be the cost of all that? How many of us are living lives we didn't choose for ourselves, simply because we were told that this is the way things "should" be? How many dreams have died because they didn't fit into society's idea of normal? How many of us wear masks to live up to these expectations, creating dual personalities—one for the world to see, and one that remains hidden for fear of what others might think of them?

I've seen this struggle in many of the clients I've coached. I once had a client who wasn't happy with the career she was allowed to have. Working in mixed environments was a big no for the family. She wanted to learn how to be confident in herself and take action for a life and a career closer to her ambitions while also learning how to deal with setbacks and stand up for herself. Another client wanted to learn how to deal with the pressure of silencing her inner critic and setting boundaries with her extended family who were angry with her for not being married and thought she'd chosen a career for herself instead. Yet another client was miserable in her marriage but was told to stay for the sake of the kids even though her husband was abusing her emotionally and mentally. She wanted help on how she could build courage to make difficult decisions.

These clients all came with built walls around themselves because they feared being different and acting differently to what they felt was expected of them.. And when I say different, I don't even mean extreme behaviors. I'm talking about simple things such as having a unique personality, pursuing a creative passion, wanting to study something unconventional, exploring life outside the traditional education system, or being confident and vocal and standing up for what they believe in. Even these seemingly small differences can be met with resistance.

Why is it so difficult for others to accept that we are not all the same? I wholeheartedly believe that our uniqueness is something to be celebrated, not suppressed. When we try to push everyone into specific categories, we create divisions that lead to hatred, racism, and extremism. These divisions make the world a worse place to live in. Just take a look around at what's going on in the world and you'll see what I mean. We need to learn to accept our differences and still live in harmony. In the eyes of our Creator, we are all equal. Our value doesn't come from where we're from, our family name, our class, or our race—it comes from how good a person we are and what good we do in this world. That's what makes each of us unique.

So, how do we start embracing our uniqueness when we've spent our entire lives trying to fit in? The first step is to become aware of why we feel the need to conform. Is it because we want to belong? Is it because that's all we know? Is it because we're afraid to stand out, preferring to blend in and avoid the spotlight of our magic?

If you've ever felt this way, know that you're not alone. It's important to ask yourself some tough but necessary questions: Who are you when no one is looking? Who do you become when you're being your true self?

It's crucial to distinguish between who you are now and who you really are deep down. Our identities are shaped by a mix of factors, some of which we like, and some we don't. The more we dislike certain aspects of ourselves, the more it indicates that we're afraid of being true to who we are.

Once you've answered these questions, ask yourself if there are people in your life with whom you feel comfortable being yourself—no walls, no facades, just you. If there are, write their names down. If not, that's okay too.

Next, consider these people. What is it about them that makes you feel safe to be yourself? And on the flip side, what is it about other people around you that makes you feel unsafe? What do you need to feel comfortable being your true self around others?

> **Embracing your uniqueness isn't just about recognizing what makes you different, it's about celebrating it as well.**

After identifying these factors, it's time to start celebrating how different and special you are. I want you to write down ten things that make you unique, things you don't think anyone else in the world can do quite like you. These could be talents, habits, or ways of thinking that are uniquely yours.

For example, I love how I hug my sister's kids so tightly that they feel safe and secure in my arms, playing with my fingers while sitting on my lap. I love how I can make anyone feel comfortable enough to share their deepest secrets with me without feeling guilty, judged, or threatened. I love how approachable I am, not just to people who look or sound like me, but to everyone, because I embrace diversity and know how important it is to feel like you belong. I love how I can have moments of feeling like a genius, ready to conquer the world with my coaching skills, and other times when I just want to be held and cared for because I feel the weight of the world on my shoulders.

Now, it's your turn. What makes you unique? Write down those small moments that make you the real you—the different, unique, special YOU.

Embracing your uniqueness is about letting go of the need to conform to societal expectations and instead living a life that is true to who you are. It's about understanding that being different isn't something to be feared but something to be embraced. By acknowledging and celebrating our differences, we not only find our true selves but also contribute to a world that values diversity, creativity, and uniqueness, a world where we can all live in harmony, appreciating our unique contributions.

So, let's break free from the chains of normalcy. Let's step out of the ready-made molds and create our own paths. Let's be bold enough to be different, to be ourselves, and to live lives that are authentically ours.

Now, let's talk about the elephant in the room that so many dread or shy away from: shame.

I remember vividly the sting of humiliation when a relative looked me in the eye and said that I would never get married because of how much I weighed. What made it even more painful was that this comment came at a time when I had already started taking care of my health and had lost a significant amount of weight. It happened at a wedding when I had put so much effort into my appearance. I had carefully chosen my dress, spent time on my makeup and hair, and felt proud of how I looked. I was happy with the reflection in the mirror, content with the effort I had made, and most importantly, I felt good about myself and felt beautiful. Then, out of nowhere, this relative's harsh words came like a punch to the gut, triggering all the old insecurities I thought I had buried about myself and my image.

This incident is just one of many moments in my life that brought a wave of shame. I know I'm not alone in this. How many times have you found yourself biting your tongue, not speaking up because your opinion was different from those around you, and you were afraid of being judged or embarrassed? How many times have you hidden from your parents because you didn't achieve the perfect grade? How many dreams have you set aside because they didn't align with the conventional path, and you were too ashamed to pursue something that made you stand out? How many times were you ashamed to stand out and shine within your accomplishments and your hard work? How many days have you spent thinking about others' opinions and judgments if you were to just be you?

Shame is a powerful emotion. It's a topic we rarely feel comfortable discussing openly. Shame is defined as "a feeling of embarrassment or humiliation that arises from the perception of having done something dishonorable, immoral, or improper."[1] But it goes deeper than that. Shame makes us want to hide the parts of ourselves that we think are unworthy, undesirable, or different from the norm.

For many of us, shame is a constant companion, whispering in our ears that we are not enough. It tells us to keep our true selves hidden, to conform, and to avoid standing out. But shame becomes harmful when it becomes a part of our identity, when it starts to dictate our self-worth and the way we see ourselves.

So why do we feel this intense need to fit in? Is it because we crave belonging? Is it because this is all we've ever known? Is it because we fear the spotlight that comes with being different?

---

[1] Verywell Mind, "What Is Shame?" Available at: Verywell Mind

If you've ever asked yourself these questions, know that you're not alone.

Shame thrives where there is immense pressure to adhere to certain societal expectations. We are taught from a young age to follow the rules, to fit into our designated roles, and to maintain the family's honor. But what happens when these societal expectations clash with our true selves? What happens when the pressure to conform becomes so overwhelming that it stifles our dreams and aspirations?

For many women, shame is tied to our appearance, our roles, and our choices. We are made to feel ashamed if we don't fit the ideal standards of beauty that society imposes on us. We feel ashamed if we're not married by a certain age, as if our worth is tied to our marital status. We feel ashamed if we choose to pursue a career and are judged for not being there for our children every moment of the day. Conversely, we are made to feel ashamed if we choose to stay at home, as if being a full-time mother isn't a valid or valuable choice. We feel ashamed if we can't conceive or even if we delay having children when married, as if there's a certain agenda we need to follow as a woman. We feel ashamed when we ask for a divorce, as if being divorced is *haram* (forbidden).

The list goes on and on. Women feel ashamed when they earn more money than their spouses, or when they need help because they're expected to be the superwomen who can do it all, or when they pursue their dreams and refuse to settle for less than they deserve. This shame is perpetuated not just by those around us but also by the representations we see in the media—on TV, in movies, and even in the music we listen to. These messages reinforce the idea that there is a "right" way to be a woman, and anything outside of that narrow definition is something to be ashamed of.

But we need to challenge this narrative. We need to recognize that shame triggers our innate desire to belong and can make us conform to things that aren't necessarily right for us. The key difference between healthy and harmful shame lies in how we internalize it. Healthy shame might keep us from making a truly harmful decision, but harmful shame attacks our very own identity. When we start to believe that we are inherently flawed, that there is something fundamentally wrong with us, shame becomes destructive.

Let's do an exercise together. Think back to a recent moment when you felt embarrassed or humiliated. What happened? What were you telling yourself at that moment? What did it lead to?

If your self-talk included phrases like, *You're so stupid*, *You're a bad person*, or *You deserve this*, then you're dealing with harmful shame. This kind of shame is dangerous because it goes beyond the incident itself and starts to define who you are. When shame becomes who we are rather than just an emotion we feel, it starts to control our self-worth and the way we perceive ourselves.

I can recall numerous incidents when I was humiliated or embarrassed by comments about me, but because I was taught to respect my elders and not speak back, I remained silent. I was taught that family boundaries didn't exist because we are all one, and as a result, my feelings were often disregarded.

This is particularly true for those of us who have been conditioned by the "good girl" syndrome, which I will explore in the next chapter. We feel ashamed when we don't meet society's expectations, and this shame becomes a barrier to our happiness and fulfillment.

But here's the truth: Shame doesn't have to define us. We can break free from its grip. We can start by recognizing when we're feeling shame and understanding that it's not a reflection of our true worth. We can begin to question the societal norms that make us feel less than, and we can challenge the idea that we need to fit into a certain mold to be accepted.

In summary, breaking free from societal expectations and embracing our uniqueness is a journey that requires us to confront the deep-rooted beliefs that tell us we must conform to be accepted. It's about recognizing that what we consider "normal" is just a set of behaviors that society has come to accept over time. We have the power to redefine normal for ourselves, to celebrate our uniqueness rather than suppress it, and to live lives true to who we are. By challenging the shame that holds us back and by questioning the societal expectations that limit us, we open ourselves up to a world where diversity, creativity, and authenticity thrive. Ultimately, our value lies not in how well we fit into a mold but in how we use our uniqueness to make a positive impact on the world around us. And tackling the "good girl" syndrome is another way to get back to our true selves and build on our true identity of who we are, which brings us to the next chapter.

Chapter 3:
Breaking Free from the Good Girl Syndrome

One of the most profound conversations I've had with myself—and my coach, long before I became a coach—was about the pervasive "good girl" syndrome. This mindset, which affects women globally but especially in the Middle East, revolves around the belief that being loved, accepted, and valued requires being "good" all the time. But what does it really mean to be a "good girl," and how does it limit our potential and self-love?

The "good girl" syndrome is not just a social construct but also a significant barrier to personal growth. Rooted in cultural, religious, and societal norms, it dictates how women should behave, often leading to perfectionism and people-pleasing. The problem isn't with being "good" but with the unrealistic standards women are held to, standards that often lead to exhaustion, frustration, and self-doubt.

From a young age, women are conditioned to please others—parents, family, husbands, children, or society at large. This conditioning often leads to women suppressing their own needs and desires, prioritizing everyone else's happiness over their own. This people-pleasing behavior isn't just cultural; it is often reinforced by misinterpreted religious beliefs.

For example, verses from the Quran are sometimes taken out of context to support the idea that women must conform. One verse from Surah An-Nisa (4:34) is often misused to suggest that men have complete authority over women:

"الرِّجَالُ قَوَّامُونَ عَلَى النِّسَاءِ بِمَا فَضَّلَ اللَّهُ بَعْضَهُمْ عَلَى بَعْضٍ وَبِمَا أَنْفَقُوا مِنْ أَمْوَالِهِمْ"

"Men are the protectors and maintainers of women, because Allah has given the one more (strength) than the other, and because they support them from their means."

However, this verse speaks to the responsibility men have in providing for and protecting women, not diminishing their independence. It emphasizes mutual respect, not domination.

Similarly, Surah Al-Baqarah (2:228) contains the phrase "men have a degree over them," which is often cited to imply male superiority:

"وَلَهُنَّ مِثْلُ الَّذِي عَلَيْهِنَّ بِالْمَعْرُوفِ ۚ وَلِلرِّجَالِ عَلَيْهِنَّ دَرَجَةٌ ۗ وَاللَّهُ عَزِيزٌ حَكِيمٌ"

"And due to the wives is similar to what is expected of them, according to what is reasonable. But the men have a degree over them [in responsibility]."

In reality, this verse refers to men's additional financial responsibilities in marriage, not a blanket superiority. Women are granted equality in terms of rights and responsibilities.

When these verses are misinterpreted, they contribute to the "good girl" syndrome, trapping women in roles that demand perfection and compliance.

Signs of the "Good Girl" Syndrome

Women affected by this syndrome exhibit several common traits.

- **Inability to set boundaries** Women often feel they must be available to everyone, placing their own needs last. This self-sacrificing behavior leaves them emotionally and physically drained.
- **Perfectionism** The need to be the perfect wife, mother, daughter, and professional leads to constant pressure to excel in every role. This pursuit of perfection is exhausting and unachievable.
- **Difficulty saying no** Women feel guilty for prioritizing their own needs, fearing that they won't be loved if they refuse to help others, even at the cost of their own well-being.
- **Fear of expressing opinions** Fear of judgment or abandonment keeps many women from voicing their true opinion and thoughts. This repression leads to emotional turbulence, which can manifest in physical ailments over time.

Striving to meet society's impossible standards of being a "good girl" can be truly harmful and can lead to several detrimental outcomes.

- **Burnout** Constantly putting others' needs first results in physical and emotional exhaustion, where you feel like you have hit rock bottom and don't have the capacity and energy to pick yourself back up.
- **Mental health issues** Perfectionism and people-pleasing can lead to anxiety, depression, and identity crises within women. These are serious issues that cannot be neglected, because they can build up to become severe.

- **Chronic stress** Stress is no joke, and in its extreme form translates to physical pain and illness. How many times have you heard women complain about certain bodily aches they don't know the cause of? Rest assured that stress has been the issue.

Liberation from the "good girl" syndrome begins with self-awareness. Recognize the ways in which the syndrome has shaped your life and understand that you do not need to be "good" to be loved or valued.

Here are steps to start reclaiming your authenticity back to your THAT:

1. **Set boundaries.** Learn to protect your time and emotional energy by setting clear boundaries. Remember, saying no is not selfish, it's necessary for self-preservation.
2. **Challenge perfectionism.** Let go of the need to be perfect. Mistakes are part of growth, and your worth is not dependent on meeting unrealistic standards.
3. **Express your opinions.** Practice sharing your thoughts, even when they differ from others. Your voice is important and deserves to be heard.
4. **Prioritize self-care.** Make time for self-care, which is essential for your emotional and physical well-being. Caring for yourself enables you to care for others from a place of strength.
5. **Seek support.** If the pressure to conform feels overwhelming, seek guidance from a coach or therapist who can help you navigate this journey.

6. **Celebrate your uniqueness.** Embrace what makes you different. You don't need to fit into society's mold to be worthy of love and acceptance.

You're Not Alone Community Session about "Good Girl" Syndrome

During a session with the *You're Not Alone* community, we explored the "good girl" syndrome together in an open and safe discussion. We looked at what the concept meant, how it affected our self-worth, society's role in imposing such a concept, and then we looked at how can we empower ourselves to defy the norms and create boundaries for a healthier self-worth.

The session was transformative, filled with collective healing as women realized how much of their lives had been defined by unrealistic standards. Women shared how the authority of their fathers, husbands, and even sometimes brothers shaped the "good girl" syndrome in what they thought was "right." Some women raised the point that sometimes it's just the brothers rather than the fathers who imply this authority and misuse it under the misconception of what Islam permits in their role as protectors and providers. The women even heard such phrases as "ناقصات عقل و دين," which means women are missing some of their mind and religion therefore cannot have the authority to dictate how they live their lives or make choices for themselves. The surprising fact is how their mothers and older generations of women truly believed that and imprinted this thought within the male figures in their lives as well.

We also dismantled the notion of "الرجال قوامون على النساء" and how taking half verses from the Quran to present men's right to authority and control, without looking at the context of the entire verse and how it in fact empowers women, was building these wrong beliefs in their minds. At the end of the session, we did an exercise to thank ourselves for being where we are, which is exactly where we need to be, and reflecting on all the efforts women make to fight the norm, break misconceptions, and claim our authenticity and truth just as our true religion entitles us to be.

> **It was a healing circle where each of us showed up with her definition of courage and acknowledged herself for everything she was doing to connect to her true self and to always show up for herself, no matter what.**

I concluded by taking in all that was shared during the session, where each participant in turn thanked herself for where she was right then, and ended with thanking myself for never giving up on the idea of this community, despite all the rejections and struggles I went through. Seeing those women share so gracefully and be present for each other, holding space for one another, was so powerful and rewarding it made my mini-me very happy and emotional. It was tearful yet so powerful, and that's a moment I will never forget!

The "good girl" syndrome is a harmful mindset deeply ingrained in many cultures, especially in collectivist societies. But it's time to redefine what it means to be "good." True goodness isn't about pleasing others at the expense of your well-being. It's about embracing your authenticity, setting boundaries, and living a life that reflects who you truly are.

Take a moment to thank yourself for everything you've endured and overcome. You are worthy, not because of how perfectly you've conformed, but because of the courage you've shown in being your true self.

Chapter 4:
Don't Let Cultural Traditions Derail You from Religion

In this chapter I am going to tackle one of the biggest misunderstandings we have within our Middle Eastern societies—a misunderstanding that is holding back the growth and development of individuals and, more critically, driving people away from the true essence of our beautiful religion, Islam. Being raised by parents who were able to distinguish between cultural traditions and the true teachings of Islam has been the greatest gift I have ever received. I'm forever grateful for this foundation, because I've seen firsthand the effects of this confusion on the people I coach and work with.

We've all heard inspiring stories of people who revert to Islam, often with a sense of awe at how they perceive and embrace the religion. Sometimes I hear Muslims express a longing: *"Why don't I see my religion the way they do when they revert to Islam?"* My answer is always the same: *"Reintroduce yourself to Islam as if you are learning about it for the first time, and you will rediscover its beauty and justice."*

The issue is that many of us in the Middle East mainly have grown up with a version of Islam that is heavily intertwined with culture and traditions, often all lumped together under the umbrella of religion. This mixture has led to a distorted understanding of what Islam truly is. One of the most damaging aspects of this confusion is the way Islam is often presented as a religion to be feared rather than one to be loved and respected.

How many of you have grown up fearing your parents more than you fear God? How many times have you found yourself praying not out of love or devotion to the Almighty but because you feared the consequences from your family if you didn't? How many of you have internalized the belief that your relationship with God is contingent upon your obedience to your parents? You might have heard something like this when growing up: *"If you don't obey us, God will hate you."* Or: *"If you don't do as we say, God will punish you."* Or: *"If you say no to us, God will be mad with you."* These statements, drilled in from a young age, often become limiting beliefs that we carry into adulthood, hindering our spiritual growth and understanding.

The problem with this approach is that it distorts the essence of Islam. Islam is a religion of love, mercy, and justice wherein one develops a personal relationship with Allah, a relationship based on trust, understanding, and sincerity. When we reduce Islam to a set of rigid rules enforced by fear, we lose sight of this relationship. We start to see Allah as a punishing figure rather than as the Merciful Creator who understands our struggles and desires to guide us to the right path.

The Prophet Muhammad (peace be upon him) emphasized that religion should not be a burden but rather a great example of moderation in life. He said through one of the Hadiths that

"إن الدين يسر و لن يشاد الدين أحد الا غلبه، فسددوا و قاربوا و أبشروا و استعينوا بالغدوة و الروحة و شيء من الدلجة" -صحيح البخاري

Indeed Religion is easy, and no one makes the religion difficult except that it overpowers him. So aim for moderation, do your best, and rejoice, and seek help in the morning, the afternoon, and during the night (Sahih Bukhari).

Yet, when cultural traditions are imposed on us as religious obligations, they often make our practice of Islam feel heavy and difficult. We begin to associate our faith with anxiety and fear rather than with peace and contentment.

This is not to say that all traditions are bad. Many cultural practices do enrich our lives and help us connect with our communities and are there for that reason of identity. We cannot throw away the part of our identity that comes with how culture and traditions translate. However, when these practices contradict or overshadow the true teachings of our religion Islam, sometimes they can lead us astray. It's crucial that we distinguish between what is cultural and what is religious. We must strive to practice Islam as it was revealed, in its pure form, without the added weight of cultural expectations that contradict its learnings.

One of the most common areas where this confusion manifests is in the way women are treated within our societies. Cultural norms often dictate what women should do, how we should behave, and even think, and these norms are then justified in the name of religion. But if we look closely at the teachings of Islam, we find a different narrative, one that honors women, gives them rights, and protects their dignity. The Prophet Muhammad (peace be upon him) was a strong advocate for the rights of women, and he emphasized kindness, respect, and equality in his treatment of women, even specifically during his last speech خطبة الوداع (his farewell speech before his last days) when he emphasized to treat women well.

Another area where tradition often overrides true religious understanding is in how we approach marriage. In many cultures, marriage is heavily influenced by family status, financial considerations, and societal expectations, often at the expense of the spiritual and emotional compatibility of the couple. Although Islam provides guidance on choosing a spouse, it emphasizes virtue, character, and mutual respect above all else. When these criteria are sidelined in favor of cultural norms, the true purpose of marriage in Islam—to build a partnership based on love and mutual support—can be lost.

We also see this confusion in how children are raised. Many of us were brought up in environments where obedience to parents was conflated with obedience to God. Although respecting and honoring our parents is indeed a fundamental part of Islam, it should not overshadow our personal relationship with God, not being through the parent. Children should be taught to love God, not just fear Him. They should be encouraged to pray and worship out of a sense of devotion and connection, not out of fear of punishment.

The Quran itself is a guide that invites us to reflect, to think, and to understand. It doesn't ask for blind adherence to cultural norms but calls us to seek knowledge and wisdom. It encourages us to ask questions, to seek clarity, and to understand the reasons behind our beliefs and practices. This is the path to true faith—a faith that is personal, thoughtful, and sincere.

So, what can we do to untangle this mix of culture and religion? First, we need to educate ourselves about the true teachings of Islam. We need to go back to the Quran and the Hadith, to study the life of the Prophet Muhammad (peace be upon him), and to seek knowledge from scholars who understand the difference between culture and religion.

Second, we need to have open and honest conversations within our families and communities. We need to question traditions that don't align with the teachings of Islam and be brave enough to challenge them. This doesn't mean abandoning our culture but rather refining it in a way that complements our faith.

Finally, we need to nurture a personal relationship with God. This means moving beyond the fear-based practices we may have grown up with and developing a connection with God that is based on love, understanding, and trust. When we do this, we will begin to see Islam not as a set of rules to follow but as a source of peace, guidance, and joy.

In conclusion, it's time to reintroduce ourselves to Islam in its purest form. Let's strip away the cultural layers that have clouded our understanding and reconnect with the true essence of our faith. By doing so, we not only strengthen our own relationship with God but also contribute to the growth and development of our communities, helping create a society that reflects the true values of Islam: justice, mercy, and compassion.

Chapter 5:
The Voice Within: Healing Self-Talk and Embracing Self-Love

Take a moment to reflect on this question: Do you know that how we talk to ourselves is heavily influenced by how others spoke to us or to themselves when we were young and what we made of their words? Whether we received love conditionally, struggled to gain attention, or experienced trauma, these early interactions shape the beliefs we carry about ourselves—both limiting and empowering. Let's explore some of the most common scenarios we grow up with and how they can influence our internal dialogue.

- **The one who received conditional love.** You were praised and told you were loved when you achieved something or did something good: good grades, did your chores, successful moments. You heard, "That's why I love you" after accomplishments but also faced threats of rejection when you fell short: "Don't do this or I'll be mad," or "I'll love you less." This creates a self-talk pattern focused on performance, where love and approval feel earned, not simply deserved because of who you are.

- **The one who didn't get the attention they needed.** Your childhood may have been marked by seeking validation. You might have acted out, became loud or aggressive to be noticed. Or perhaps you became very quiet, bottling up your emotions and taking the back seat because that was how you were raised. This unmet need for attention can result in an ongoing struggle for external validation, where your inner voice constantly asks, *Am I enough? Do I matter?* or *Do people love me?*
- **The one who experienced childhood trauma.** Trauma, whether big or small, deeply affects how we talk to ourselves. For some, these experiences are blocked as a survival mechanism and tucked away in files within our mind that can take years to revisit (or for some people, never revisited). This can lead to limiting beliefs that feel unexplainable as well as reflexes that translate through the body as well. Trauma shapes self-perception, often resulting in inner criticism and confusion. People affected by trauma one way or the other find themselves saying things such as, "I don't know why I'm like this," "I don't remember much of my past," or have a lot of "I don't knows" in their conversations. With clients, I sometimes explore this if they are ready, but for deeper complex trauma, I recommend seeing a therapist for further support as this would cross the line and is not part of my responsibility as a coach.

When we look at how these aspects of our upbringing shape our internal dialogue, we become aware of how harsh and negative our self-talk can be. The irony is, we would never talk to someone we love the way we often talk to ourselves. When we turn into our own worst critics, constantly focusing on our flaws, it becomes harder and harder to find self-love. This critical inner voice can feel like a black hole that's difficult to escape.

But the first step into shifting this dynamic of how we speak to ourselves is acceptance.

Why is it that we can accept the flaws of others but struggle to accept our own? We tell others it's okay when things don't work out, yet we blame ourselves for the same. We criticize our every word, reaction, and appearance in ways we would never do to others.

Acceptance means embracing all of ourselves, not just the good parts. Each of us is made up of different parts, and in coaching, we often work with those parts to help them function together in harmony.

When we accept all our parts, our internal voice shifts from one of criticism to one of empowerment.

Rather than criticizing yourself, what if you spoke to yourself with love? What if you became your own best friend instead of your worst enemy?

Here's an exercise: Imagine you're not you but rather your best friend. Write down what you would say to yourself if you made a mistake or have failed. What tone of voice would you use? How would you comfort yourself? Write it all down, then read the letter back as if it were meant for you.

This exercise helps distinguish between critiquing to improve versus criticizing to bring yourself down. Learning this distinction helps shift your self-talk to a more loving, productive place.

The difference between critiquing to improve and criticizing to bring yourself down lies in the intent and outcome of the feedback you give yourself.

- **Critiquing to improve:** This type of self-talk is constructive and is focused on growth. It's about recognizing areas where you can do better and offer yourself guidance on how to improve. When you critique yourself, it's done from a place of love, encouragement, and self-respect. The goal is to help you become the best version of yourself while maintaining your self-worth.
- **Criticizing to bring yourself down:** This, on the other hand, is destructive and focused on blame or punishment. Criticism in this sense is harsh and judgmental, often coming from a place of fear, insecurity, or shame. It magnifies mistakes and flaws, leading to feelings of inadequacy or failure. When you criticize yourself, the intent is not to grow but to reinforce negative beliefs about yourself.

Kindness to yourself begins with your internal dialogue. It's about accepting all of you and treating yourself as you would a dear friend. What you practice on yourself determines what you can give to others.

By learning to distinguish between these two, you can shift your self-talk to be more loving and productive. Instead of tearing yourself down, you focus on how you can improve while still showing yourself kindness and understanding.

Self-love has long been seen as "selfish," but this couldn't be further from the truth. The concept of self-love is rooted in deep spiritual wisdom. As it says in the Quran, Surah Ar-Ra'd (13:11),

"إِنَّ اللَّهَ لَا يُغَيِّرُ مَا بِقَوْمٍ حَتَّىٰ يُغَيِّرُوا مَا بِأَنْفُسِهِمْ"

Which translates to *Indeed, Allah will not change the condition of a people until they change what is within themselves.*

The transformation you seek in your life begins within you, and loving yourself means realizing that you are here for a purpose only you can fulfill, which is done through the change you need to seek within you. It's about accepting who you are right now while working toward who you want to become.

Let me share my own story. For years, I lived disconnected from my true self, addicted to people-pleasing, basing my own worthiness of love on others' opinions, not knowing how to love myself for who I was. I was in a continuous spiral of doubting and questioning my worth. This translated into habits of strong self-criticizing, self-loathing, emotional eating, hiding my light, and being someone far from who I truly was. It wasn't until I began working with a coach that I realized my true worth, that I am enough just the way I am, and that my looks don't define who I am but learning to be all of me does. I learned to embrace every part of me and find my own blend of amazingness. I learned not to be ashamed of my culture blends (being brought up in two different countries) or feeling triggered or ashamed when I spoke in English with an American accent. I had spent much of my life undermining my value and prioritizing others' needs, and I finally confronted all those different, long-buried feelings and released what wasn't serving me.

Loving yourself means showing up for yourself every day, accepting your humanness, and recognizing that you are whole just as you are. You will always be a work in progress, and that's something to celebrate, not criticize.

Once you understand your own worth, you become a force of nature. You become aware of how you feel, how you react, and what truly matters to you. Awareness is 80 percent of the work as we said and structured this book to be. The remaining 20 percent is deciding what to do with that awareness, and from that you decide which steps you'll take toward becoming the person you want to be, one step closer every day to your THAT.

When you start loving yourself, your need for external validation diminishes. You become invested in yourself, and that energy is magnetic. People who aren't aligned with this new version of you may disappear, but others who share your values will enter your life, forming stronger personal and professional relationships. You'll let go of what no longer serves you and make space for what fulfills you.

Loving yourself isn't just about how you feel in relationships. It's also about how you do everything, from waking up to praying to interacting with family to pursuing your passions. When love is the foundation, everything changes. When you hold space for yourself and love who you are, you extend that same grace to others.

> **This is the essence of not loving oneself: putting everyone else's needs before your own and minimizing your presence in your OWN life.**

When you love yourself unconditionally, you give others the permission to do the same. It's a cycle that starts within and ripples outward. So, take that first step. Be honest with yourself, work on yourself, and only then will you be able to fully show up for others. The ripple effect of change is what inspired the logo for my company, Asmaa Consultancy. When you start with yourself in the center of your life, and seek the change you want, you become like a drop in the river. No matter how big or small the drop, its ripple effect does change the water around it, and that change within always creates a positive change outward, going up and up.

In the end, self-love isn't selfish. It's necessary. It allows you to accept yourself, grow, and become the best version of yourself. And as you learn to love yourself, you'll find that your relationships with others will transform too.

You cannot truly love others until you first learn to love yourself.

Chapter 6:
Take Care of Yourself Before You Take Care of Others

Before you start reading this chapter there is something I need you to let go of: your ego! Yes, your ego. We're here to talk to your true self, not your ego self, because that's the only way you'll be inspired by this chapter and create the awareness you need to be your true THAT.

How do you know what your ego self is and what your true self is? Let's do a quick exercise together to learn how to distinguish both voices.

If you find yourself saying things such as
- *I'm not good enough to succeed in this project*, or
- *What will people think if I fail?* or
- *I have to prove myself to everyone...*

...then it's most likely your ego-self talking. This voice judges, criticizes, and looks externally for validation, prioritizing others' opinions over your own inner truth.

But if you find yourself saying things like
- *I am capable and worthy, regardless of the outcome*, or
- *My value is not determined by others' opinions*, or
- *I can do my best and learn from the experience...*

...then that would be your THAT, your true self. Your true self is calmer, wiser, and seeks value from within rather than outside.

Leave your ego at the door. Allow yourself to be vulnerable and true as you continue reading, focusing internally on you.

Let's talk about something we, as women, often don't want to admit. Many of us were raised to be caregivers, always doing everything for everyone while keeping a smile on our faces. In chapter 3, I discussed the "good girl" syndrome, where women are socialized to be selfless at the expense of their own needs. Today, however, the role of women has expanded far beyond caregiving. We are now leaders, business owners, professionals, and much more. Although these opportunities are wonderful, they also come with a heavier load of responsibilities. The contradiction lies in expecting women to perform their expanded roles without any change in how we care for ourselves.

This constant juggling leads many women to mental, emotional, and physical exhaustion. Often, this breakdown happens because we've been conditioned to believe that our own needs are the least important. Just writing this makes me take a deep breath. We endure so much for the sake of others that we start to dismiss the very idea of taking care of ourselves. Many of us hold the belief that self-care is selfish.

You have no idea how often I've spoken to women who avoid taking care of themselves for fear of being labeled "selfish." These women are more comfortable being called selfless, sacrificing themselves for everyone else. But the truth is, selfless and selfish are intertwined.

For a long time, I thought being selfless meant being loved and accepted. I took care of others because I believed it made me feel good about myself and loved by others. But what it was really doing was draining me, because my acts of service weren't reciprocated. I had the unspoken expectation that others would appreciate what I was doing, but when that didn't happen, I began to question my own worth.

Here's an example: You go out of your way to help someone, canceling your own plans, expecting nothing in return. But when you ask for help, you're met with excuses such as, "I'm too busy," or "You can handle it yourself." Over time, this imbalance chips away at your self-worth, especially if you've always been independent and found it difficult to ask for help in the first place.

Here's something to think about: The key to being selfless is in fact being selfish.

This is the kind of situation I was in. I was burying my feelings, focusing entirely on others, and disregarding my own boundaries, just to be accepted. My relationship with myself deteriorated, and I started to question every relationship I had. I silenced my inner voice to the point that, when it finally spoke, it was filled with fire and rage.

I kept pushing down those feelings until one small, unrelated incident made all the bottled-up rage come out. That's what happens when you aren't true to yourself and fail to communicate how you really feel.

Growing up, I believed that if I shared my feelings, people would leave me. This belief was rooted in childhood, and it shaped much of how I navigated life. These were some of the limiting beliefs I formed:

- If you want to be appreciated, you need to be there for others.
- Putting yourself first means you're selfish and uncaring, which makes you a bad person.
- If you speak your mind, people won't want to be around you because you're being rude.

For years, I minimized my struggles, thinking no one would understand them. It wasn't until I found a coach who seemed to live inside my head that I understood why I was prioritizing others and not myself.

Here's part of how that conversation went:
Coach: ...and how does that make you feel?
Me: I feel lost, alone... like I'm swimming in a never-ending ocean. On one hand, I'm swimming for my life, but at the same

time, I'm tired of swimming against the waves and just want to lie back and go wherever the waves take me.
Coach: And what's holding you back from doing that?
Me: ...I guess me! I'm stopping myself from just letting go and trusting that things will work out if I focus on my own needs.

That moment helped me realize that I was holding myself back by trying to please others. It was time to let go of control and trust in *Tawakkul*—true reliance on Allah.

At that point in my career, I faced a lot of criticism for choosing coaching as a profession. I felt discouraged, but when I reflected, I saw that I was still prioritizing others' opinions over my own. I needed to let go, trust Allah, and stop trying to control every detail.

Tawakkul means trusting in Allah's plan after you've done your part. It's about letting go of the need to control everything and having faith that Allah will take care of you. This belief gave me the strength to move forward in my coaching career, knowing that my journey was part of a greater plan.

When I started putting myself first, I realized that I was able to give more to others. By filling my own cup, I could give out of abundance, not scarcity. Giving from an empty cup, driven by the need for external validation, leads to frustration. But giving from a full cup, driven by self-love, leads to joy and fulfillment.

So, is taking care of yourself selfish? Yes, it is, but in the best possible way. It's the key to being selfless and giving to others from a place of strength and love.

Taking care of yourself means knowing your limits, setting boundaries, and loving yourself enough to prioritize your needs.

> **Taking care of yourself in another definition means discipline.**

It all starts with your mindset and the story you tell yourself about who you are and what you deserve.

In one of our *You're Not Alone* sessions, one of my guests of honor highlighted the importance of self-discipline. Many people interpret self-love as an excuse to be lenient with themselves, but true self-love means showing up for yourself every day, even when it's hard.

Self-discipline is about being consistent and holding yourself accountable, whereas self-sabotage stems from the critic voice in your head. Learning to distinguish between the two is crucial to avoiding self-sabotage and fostering personal growth.

The key is learning to quiet the critic voice and let your true self lead. The critic voice can alert you to areas for improvement, but it should never control you. By fostering discipline instead of criticism, you can achieve your goals without tearing yourself down.

I remember going through that battle at one point. I had applied for an MC job that I was genuinely excited about. I worked hard, rehearsed diligently, and aced the rehearsal. I knew deep down that I had done a fantastic job, and I felt confident in my abilities. But when I didn't get the job, something inside me shifted. Rather than recognizing that I had done my best and that sometimes things aren't meant to be, I began to spiral into self-sabotage.

Instead of empowering myself by acknowledging the effort and talent I had put into the audition, I let that rejection define my self-worth. I started questioning everything: whether I was good enough, whether I even had the skills to continue in this field, and whether I would ever succeed. The rejection took over my thoughts, and instead of being a reminder of the resilience and courage I had shown in putting myself out there, it became an excuse to criticize myself and second-guess my value.

What I failed to realize at that moment was that rejection doesn't equate to failure or inadequacy. Just because I didn't get that specific job didn't mean I wasn't capable, and it certainly didn't diminish my worth. Looking back, I see how much of my self-sabotage stemmed from allowing external circumstances to dictate my internal value. If I had reminded myself of my effort and abilities, I could have used that rejection as a steppingstone toward future opportunities, rather than letting it pull me down into a spiral of doubt.

That experience taught me a valuable lesson: No matter how much we excel or how much effort we put in, the outcome isn't always what we hope for. But that doesn't mean we are any less capable or worthy. And the need to juggle between your worth and love and between ways to improve is truly dependent on disciplining yourself and your inner talk.

When you find this balance between self-care and self-discipline, you'll not only grow into the best version of yourself but also be able to give more to those around you.

Remember: You are the most important person in your life. Taking care of yourself is not selfish, it's the foundation for everything else. Balance self-discipline with self-care, and trust in Allah's plan as you move forward in your journey.

Chapter 7:
Embrace The Unknown: Lessons from Life's Unplanned Turns

Easier said than done. That's probably what crossed your mind when you read the title of this chapter. How much simpler would life be if we had the power to control everything and everyone? We'd dictate our fate, determine how people treated us, what they thought of us, where we lived... We'd control the weather, end wars, stop evil, and choose the family we were born into. We'd shape the world to fit the perfect life we envision.

But the truth is, so much is beyond our control, and if we were to choose our fate all over again, having seen other people's fates and struggles and where we end up, we would choose our own. It's tempting to think that controlling the external world would allow us to control our lives. I remember when I first started coaching, I believed that if I could control people's perception of me, they would trust me enough to become my clients. I became what I now call a "fake" coach, creating an image of perfection, promising results I couldn't always guarantee. When I started, I overpromised both my clients and myself about what we'd achieve, and that spiraled into not being present during sessions and not showing the true essence of coaching, which can be transformative when done right. Looking back, I was so focused on what others thought of me that I couldn't provide the value my clients deserved. I was disconnected, stuck in my head, and lost focus on being present in their journey and within the sessions. This is what happens when you focus on what you cannot control.

When we obsess over things beyond our control, we lose touch with the present and either get stuck in the past or preoccupied with the future. Living in the past can lead us into a cycle of self-blame. We start to dwell on how things could have gone differently or what we should have done to achieve a better outcome.

Self-blame is like poison. When we blame ourselves for every choice or mistake, we amplify the critic voice in our heads. And yes, we all have multiple voices in our minds, and no, that doesn't mean we're crazy. There are many facets to who we are, each with its own voice. When the critic speaks, it says things such as, *Why did you say that? You're not good enough. You're crazy. You're worthless.* It corners us in our own minds. Imagine being in a dark room with a spotlight over your head, crouched in a corner while this critical voice scolds you. That's how I imagined my critic voice the first time I discussed this with my own coach.

I shared this image with my coach, and together we explored why I was doing this to myself—constantly criticizing my past choices. Over time, I realized that this critic voice was a reflection of my mother's voice from my childhood. I have a great relationship with her, and I love her deeply, but growing up, I always tried to be the perfect child. I never wanted to give her a reason to be upset with me, as I had seen her react to my siblings when they didn't listen. My need for perfection was driven by a desire to win her approval and love. The critic voice in my head had been keeping that need alive, telling me that if I wasn't perfect, I wouldn't be loved.

Writing this realization now brings a fresh wave of insight. Self-blame often starts with what we internalized about ourselves in childhood. Our subconscious stores these experiences, and when we venture outside of our comfort zone or try to assert ourselves, the critic kicks in as a survival mechanism to keep us "safe." However, safety in this sense comes at the cost of growth, and when self-blame becomes a comfort zone, it's difficult to escape. But the truth is, we can never control what others think of us. Dwelling in the past does far more harm than good.

On the other hand, some people fixate on the future as another form of control. Afraid of the unknown, they plan for every possible outcome, trying to prepare for every scenario. For others, focusing on the future is a way to distract themselves from their present struggles. Both are rooted in fear—fear of failure, judgment, success, or even death.

The problem with living in the future is that it keeps us from being present. The only moment we truly have is the present. We have no idea what the future holds or whether we'll even be alive to see it. Overthinking has become a modern affliction, contributing to anxiety and depression.

I remember the anxiety I felt when deciding whether to step into the public eye as a coach in Qatar. It wasn't an easy decision for several reasons. First, I come from a conservative extended family, and they viewed this kind of career as unnecessary, worrying about what others would think. Second, we live in a conservative, collectivistic small society that isn't always open to change or new ideas. I was anxious about how I would be perceived. What would people think? Would they like me? Would I get hate? Was this the right move? What if I failed and became the subject of gossip?

I spent a long time reflecting on these thoughts, only to realize that everything I was worried about was out of my control. Whether people liked me or not, how I was perceived, or whether I would fail, none of it was up to me. I wouldn't know the answers unless I tried, and only then could I decide my next move.

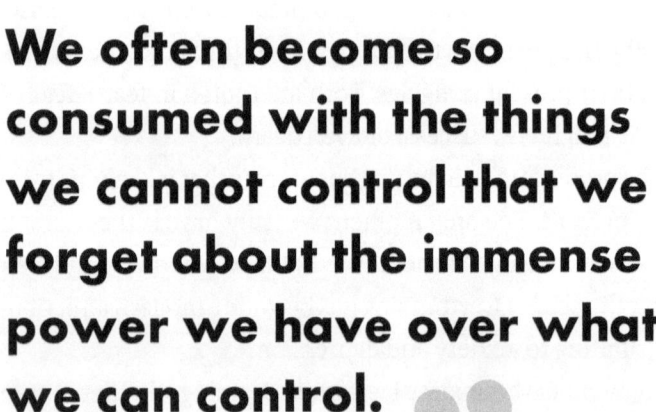

We often become so consumed with the things we cannot control that we forget about the immense power we have over what we can control.

We have control over our thoughts, our reactions, our emotions, and how we relate to others. We decide who stays in our lives and who doesn't. We control how we view and present ourselves to the world. We dictate the energy we put out and how we allow others to influence us. Most important, we control our actions in the present moment.

So, as you read this, think about what you can control right now. How do you want to spend this moment? Do you want to be consumed by anxiety and overthink things that are beyond your reach? Or do you want to focus on what you can control, stepping into your power and living as the best version of yourself?

Not long ago, I was journaling and reflecting about a frustration I had. Something I worked very hard on hadn't turned out the way I expected. I had poured my heart into a course I believed in, but when it came time to launch, the registration numbers were disappointing. I found myself dissecting every little detail, wondering if I had missed something or if I could have done better. The reality is, sometimes we'll never have all the answers, and that is okay.

Letting go is easier said than done, especially when we crave control. We want to know what went wrong to avoid making the same mistake again. We want to protect ourselves from disappointment, failure, and pain. But no matter how much we prepare, life throws us into situations we never could have anticipated.

Imagine living in a world where everything was predetermined, where success was guaranteed and failure nonexistent. It might sound appealing at first, because who wouldn't want to avoid mistakes? But when I think about it, a life without uncertainty feels flat and uninteresting. Without challenges, without the unknown, there's no space for growth. We wouldn't discover new strengths or uncover hidden aspects of ourselves.

It's the difficult moments—the struggles, the failures—that shape us the most. They push us to confront our limits and force us to dig deep to find resilience. These moments teach us who we really are and what we truly want.

When I think back to my experience with the course, I realize that the disappointment wasn't just about the low numbers but about something deeper: my fear that my effort wasn't enough, that perhaps I wasn't enough. But after reflecting, I understood that this experience was not a measure of my worth. It was an opportunity to reassess, to learn, and to grow.

We often believe success is a straight line, but it's not. The path to success is winding, full of detours, dead ends, and unexpected turns. Every step, even the setbacks, is part of the journey. These detours aren't distractions, they're scenic routes offering some of the best views if we're willing to look. I always use this metaphor with my clients during sessions: Life is like the path of a heartbeat. It has its ups and downs, but if it didn't, we wouldn't be alive, feel alive, and that's why life is beautiful with all its ups and downs because it makes us feel alive from within.

Knowing what you don't want can be just as valuable as knowing what you do. Every failure holds a lesson. That's not to trivialize the pain that comes with failure—some disappointments cut deep—but if we shift our perspective and see the good in every situation, we'll uncover the hidden lessons.

As I reflect on my journey, I see that every mistake played a crucial role in getting me where I am today. If my first business hadn't failed, I wouldn't have discovered my passion for coaching. If some relationships hadn't ended, I wouldn't have

> **The key to embracing the unknown is learning not to fear it but to lean into it.**

learned my self-worth or begun the healing process. If my father hadn't refused to let me study abroad for my master's in a subject I wasn't happy about, I wouldn't have found my love for digital humanities and this new field, a field I not only excel in but also deeply cherish.

And it's not just the big events. Each everyday frustration—the course that didn't sell, the client who didn't sign up, the idea that didn't take off—is an opportunity to learn and pivot. These moments remind us that success isn't about avoiding failure but embracing it as part of the process.

Life often works out in ways we didn't expect. The unknown is where the most valuable lessons are found. We don't know what the future holds or where God will lead us, but we can trust that whatever path we're on is the right one for us. God's plans are always better than ours, even if we can't see it at that moment.

It's easy to look back and focus on what didn't go as planned—the missed opportunities, the failures, the "what ifs." But what if, instead, we choose to focus on the lessons learned? Each setback can be a steppingstone, each failure a building block, each no a redirection toward something better.

There's a freedom that comes with letting go of the need to control everything. It's the freedom to explore, to take risks, to fail, and to know that failure isn't the end but just another step forward.

Even when the future is uncertain, even when the outcome is unclear, we're exactly where we need to be. Each experience shapes us, helps us grow, and prepares us for what's ahead.

So, what's our role in all of this? Simple: Keep moving forward, keep trying, and keep working to become the best version of yourself. We can't control the how, when, or who, but the sooner we accept that, the sooner we'll find peace in our journey.

Let go of the need to control every outcome, and you'll open yourself to possibilities you never imagined. Life becomes less about avoiding failure and more about embracing growth. Challenges become steppingstones to something greater.

In the end, every no, every rejection, every uncertainty leads you closer to where you're meant to be. Keep journaling, keep reflecting, and keep moving forward, trusting that the unknown holds something beautiful for you. The things that don't work out are just as important as the ones that do. They're the moments that push us to grow and remind us that life isn't about having all the answers but about having the courage to keep going even when we don't.

Chapter 8:
Don't Give Up On Your Dreams: You're Not Born to Be NORMAL!

Have you ever wondered where your dreams and aspirations come from? Have you ever sat down and asked yourself why you want to achieve all those dreams? This question has crossed my mind countless times. As a child, my dreams always seemed bigger than the reality I lived in. I often questioned why I believed I could achieve such grand things.

It wasn't until I explored the nature of creativity and the concept of destiny that I began to understand the true significance of our dreams. According to Elizabeth Gilbert in her book *Big Magic*, our ideas, dreams, and solutions to problems exist for a reason. They are not random but rather creative forces seeking to be realized. Gilbert suggests that these ideas are like living entities, searching for the right mind to bring them into the world. If you don't act on your ideas, they may move on to someone else who is ready to bring them to life.

Think of your mind as a magnetic field, drawing in ideas and dreams like scattered papers. The moment you take action, these ideas begin to take shape, evolving from mere thoughts into tangible realities. This is how every successful venture begins—not just with a dream but with the courage to act on it.

Sometimes you just need to remind yourself that you are capable. In times of doubt, I find immense comfort in the verse from the Quran, "ا يكلف الله نفساً الا وسعها," which translates to "God does not burden any soul beyond its capability." This verse serves as a powerful reminder that our dreams and aspirations are not beyond our reach. They are placed in our hearts and minds because we have the potential to achieve them. God would not give you a dream you are incapable of realizing and achieving. Take a moment to reflect on this piece of information, because it really gives you the boost of confidence and reassurance that you are capable of achieving what you have in your head if you set your mind and work toward it.

This perspective shifts the focus from *Can I achieve this?* to *I am capable of achieving this*. Your dreams are not random; they are perfectly aligned with your strengths, your journey, and your destiny.

There is a great deal of psychological research that supports the idea that our dreams reflect our deepest desires and untapped potential. Studies indicate that having aspirations is closely linked to increased motivation, resilience, and overall life satisfaction. When we aim high, we push ourselves beyond our perceived limits, unlocking capabilities we might not have known we possessed. The "self-fulfilling prophecy" theory highlights the importance of believing in our dreams. If you believe that you can achieve something, your actions will align with that belief, making success more likely. And that is the motive for writing this book and getting you back to your THAT.

On the other hand, if you doubt your ability to succeed, your actions may subconsciously undermine your efforts, leading to failure. This is why it is crucial to believe in yourself and in your dreams, because your mindset can shape your reality. The strength of our beliefs is not just a motivational idea but is backed by research that shows how deeply our expectations influence our outcomes. When we dream big, we give ourselves permission to explore beyond our current limitations, allowing new possibilities to emerge. That's why writing down your dreams and goals as if you have already achieved them gives you a higher probability of achieving them. That is why vision boards work. That is why setting SMART goals and steps truly help you achieve your goals. More on that in the second part of the book.

We all experience moments when the voices around us (sometimes from those we love) urge us to lower our expectations, to play it safe, or even to abandon our dreams altogether. I've had family members say to me, "Who are you to achieve such things? Just stay ordinary, like the rest of us." It's disheartening to hear such words, especially from those we expect to support us.

However, these voices often reflect their own fears and limitations, not ours, which is important to remember so you don't take such sayings personally. People project their insecurities onto others because it's easier than confronting their own unfulfilled potential. They may have given up on their dreams, so they discourage you from pursuing yours. But you don't have to accept their path as your own.

Use these moments of doubt as fuel. Every time someone says you can't, remind yourself that you can. Every time someone doubts you, reaffirm your belief in yourself. These moments are not setbacks. They are opportunities to strengthen your resolve and commitment to your dreams. Think of these challenges as refining tools, sharpening your vision and determination to make your dreams a reality.

When I started as a coach in Qatar back in 2018, I was one of the few coaches who went public with their services and promoted myself on social media as a Qatari. My goal was to connect with potential clients and showcase this profession that wasn't well known at that time. I particularly wanted to present myself as a coach from the same background and culture as my target clients. To put your face out there as a coach, as a local Qatari, and as a young woman, was difficult and took a lot of courage. And if that wasn't enough, I was talking and showcasing so many taboo issues in society, such as marriage, women's roles, breaking barriers, and so much more. It took a toll on me, because it was a change that not many people were ready for, which triggered many of them. I had people telling me to close my account, I had people threaten to come for me, I had people blaming me for making their girls and women stronger and more aware, I had people call me a feminist (to them, that was a bad thing, but I was honored to be called that). I had family members telling me to remove some posts because they didn't fit with our traditions and culture, and the list goes on and on. But even though it was by far one of the most difficult battles I faced, my drive to stay standing and my drive to create the change for people kept me going. Whenever someone would tell me that I could not talk about a particular topic, I would remind myself that that topic was exactly what needed to be addressed and discussed. Whenever someone told me I could not do something, I would tell myself that I could and that I was capable of doing it. Whenever someone told me to not dream big, I amplified my goals list even more to fit my dreams and aspirations. I took the negativity and used it as fuel. I always believed the more haters you have toward what you do, that more you know you are doing something right and are on the right path. That in itself is the most reassuring thing I keep in mind.

Choosing to settle for a "normal" life, as some might suggest, is not the easier path, it's just the more familiar one. But familiarity often comes with a cost: the loss of growth. Living a life that falls short of your potential creates an internal conflict, a constant tug-of-war between the person you are and the person you've allowed yourself to become. It's an ongoing battle that really takes a toll on you mentally and physically. It sets your body in perpetual fight-or-flight mode, and you forget what it feels like to be in harmony mentally.

I have seen what conforming to normal does to someone and what living your uniqueness shifts in your life. Not only in me but also within my clients. I can sense it when they come into a session, and it's a marvelous thing to experience as a coach. How one person can go from being closed down, with no confidence even in their own thoughts, holding back, being afraid of being judged, to becoming someone who comes to the session leading with their thoughts, knowing what they want to explore and address because now they are confident in themselves to become a better version of themselves and live a life truer to their own THAT. Witnessing someone finding their own spark in life is a blessing and an honor.

Remember that this journey of embracing your uniqueness is not limited by geography, culture, or religion. It is a universal truth that transcends all boundaries. No matter where you are from or what beliefs you hold, the need to reconnect with your THAT is a fundamental part of the human experience. It is about finding your true self amidst the noise of societal expectations and cultural norms.

Different cultures may have different standards of what is considered "normal," but the underlying principle remains the same: Suppressing your uniqueness to fit into those standards ultimately leads to a loss of self. It is only by embracing your true nature, your THAT, that you can live a life of authenticity and purpose.

Conforming to societal norms may offer a sense of security at first, but it comes at a great cost. This comes from experience, trust me. When you strive to be like everyone else, you lose sight of who you truly are. That is exactly what happened to me. I shared my story in a TED X talk when I spoke of my journey to overcoming self-doubt and learning to embrace imperfections as a source of strength rather than weakness. I explored how society often pushes us toward an unrealistic pursuit of perfection, but it's our flaws that make us unique and human. By shifting the narrative around failure and vulnerability, I emphasized the importance of self-acceptance, resilience, and being fearless in the face of our imperfections. Ultimately, I encouraged the audience to embrace their authentic selves and live boldly without fear of judgment. (You can watch my talk on YouTube titled "Flawed and Fearless: Embracing Imperfection.") This loss of identity can lead to feelings of emptiness, dissatisfaction, and a sense that something is missing from your life. It can also stifle your creativity and limit your potential, because you are constantly trying to fit into a mold that was never designed for you.

And did you know that conformity breeds mediocrity? When everyone is trying to be the same, innovation and progress come to a halt. The world needs diverse thinkers, people who are not afraid to challenge the status quo and bring new ideas to the table. We as humans are created on this earth to build it. "قال تعالى "هو أنشأكم من الأرض و استعمركم فيها" (هود: ٦١). By embracing your uniqueness, you contribute to the richness of human experience and help drive society forward.[2]

Remember that finding your THAT is not a one-time event. It is a lifelong journey of self-discovery and self-building. It requires you to explore different experiences, reflect on your values and beliefs, and continually grow as a person. The journey is not always easy, but it is essential for living a life that is true to who you are.

Along the way, you will face challenges and setbacks. There will be times when you are tempted to conform, to take the easier path. But it is in these moments that you must remember the importance of your THAT. Embracing your uniqueness is not just about being different for the sake of it. It is about being true to yourself, living a life that is aligned with your values, passions, and purpose of why you exist in this world.

Over time, this internal conflict manifests as dissatisfaction, regret, and a deep longing for something more. You may try to suppress these feelings, but they will continue to resurface, urging you to confront the reality of your unfulfilled potential. The discomfort of staying small is far greater than the challenges of pursuing your dreams. The emotional toll of living beneath

---

2 Clements, P. (2024, April 28). *What is individuality?* The Conducts of Life. https://theconductsoflife.com/what-is-individuality/

your potential can affect your well-being, relationships, and overall life satisfaction.

The fact that you are reading this book indicates that there is a part of you that refuses to settle, or it can be the need to stop this internal battle and find the harmony and peace within.

Your dreams are in your head for a reason. They reflect what you are capable of achieving. But to bring them to life, you must first believe that you deserve the best. Silence the inner critic that tells you otherwise. Recognize that your dreams are your destiny calling you to step into your greatness.

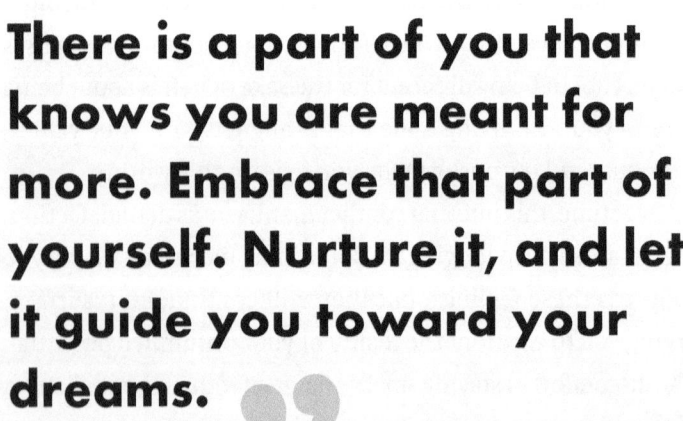

There is a part of you that knows you are meant for more. Embrace that part of yourself. Nurture it, and let it guide you toward your dreams.

In the end, being different is not just a fact of life but a beautiful aspect of our existence. It is what makes us human, what makes life interesting and worth living. By letting go of the need to be normal and embracing your THAT, you open yourself to a life of authenticity, fulfillment, and endless possibilities. This journey is universal, applicable to everyone, no matter where they are from or what they believe. It is a call to embrace your uniqueness, to live boldly, and to contribute your irreplaceable voice to the world.

Chapter 9:
We're All Afraid, but What Are YOU Going to Do About That?

Have you ever been so afraid or anxious that you would have done anything to escape that feeling, and yet you just sat there and did nothing? Or you've distracted yourself by going and hiding somewhere and then blaming yourself for not doing anything? Or even worse, started screaming at someone who had nothing to do with your situation or feelings? Yep, that's fear for you!

Everyone on this planet is afraid in one way or another. Did you know that the top fears we feel—which hold us back from becoming the people we dream of being—are fear of failure, fear of success, fear of the unknown, fear of what others might say (fear of being judged), fear of being alone, and fear of public speaking? (Yes, people fear public speaking more than death.) I'm sure you can relate to at least one of those. For me, even writing them down brings back memories of how these fears held me back from pursuing my dreams and being true to myself. I felt fear when I started coaching. I felt fear when I was comparing myself to the success of other coaches. I felt fear the first time I recorded a video for my Instagram. I felt fear when I said yes to a project I had no idea about. I felt fear when I presented my first corporate training to one of the biggest organizations in Qatar. Fear is always there, and that is something we need to admit.

I found myself stuck while writing this book and got worried that I wouldn't be able to finish it, because of all my doubts about whether it will succeed or not. That's fear creeping in. So many feelings arise, the perfectionist mentality surfaces, and that often pushes me toward procrastination. Here is a scenario of what sometimes goes on in my head when fear lingers.

One part of me says

I know you're afraid, and it's normal to be afraid of doing something new. But remember this is something you've wanted to do for so long, and you're so committed to wanting to help others. So let's pull it together and do this.

Another part of me says

I'm just too scared because of the feeling of being down right now, and I don't want those negative thoughts to make it onto the pages of this book, so maybe I shouldn't write anything until I feel motivated and positive.

Then the first voice in my head replies

Well, Asmaa, you won't always feel motivated to write the book. Focus on consistency over motivation. That's how you'll finish what you've started, especially with the deadline you've set for yourself. You can do this, and you've been through a similar situation before. Remember how you felt once you were done!

Then the other voice pipes up again and says
But you need to relax and do nothing, because why should you stress yourself out? You've been working too hard and you deserve a break (even though deep down I know I haven't been working that hard, it's just the lazier part of me talking).

But then I heard the first voice because it was my true voice, my inner leader, that truly knew what's best for me and knew what I needed to do. And as a result, I was able to finish this chapter.

Talk about a mix of emotions! Sometimes I truly don't know which voice will win the battle until I take on both voices and hear them out till the end. This is what in coaching we call parts work.

This reminds me of a question raised by one of the ladies during a session in the *You're Not Alone* community. She asked our guest which voice to listen to when coping with mom guilt and motivating herself to overcome laziness to work out. The response was insightful. She introduced the concept of "good self-blame," which I'll call the "self-discipline voice." This voice can sound kind of like the critical voice inside your head, but it's actually the one that wants you to excel, that recognizes your potential and power. So, this voice candidly points out when you didn't perform to standard, if you failed, or if you didn't meet your goal. It becomes the voice that instructs you, encourages you to rise, and drives you toward your aspirations. For me that was the first voice in the scenario just described.

How to deal with this voice can differ from one person to another but is influenced by the self-awareness you develop and how you perceive yourself. This involves connecting with your inner leader, which serves as your compass and represents the voice of your truth. And this is exactly what it means to feel the fear and do it anyway.

If we go back to the full mental scenario and try to dissect it one piece at a time, you'll see that there was a voice of fear holding me back from writing this chapter. (The irony of the title isn't lost on me.) Fear of failure and fear of what others might think about my book and my writing skills are the real reasons I felt uninspired and demotivated and procrastinated about writing. At the same time, the voice of reason, or what I like to call my inner leader, was not settling for those excuses and was holding me accountable for my goals and dreams.

It's so scary to do something new! Everyone has been through it at some point, whether in a new school, new friends, new workplace, new relationships, or a new business. Whatever it may be, that fear of not knowing what to expect, or whether you'll be accepted for who you are, or whether you will succeed, can hold you back from experiencing and even showing up as yourself.

You don't need to be perfect to take the first step. You'll never be fully prepared for the journey ahead. You can never predict what will happen, no matter how hard you try to set plans to shield yourself from potential setbacks.

We all experience the emotion of fear in our day-to-day lives, but what distinguishes you from anyone else in this world is how you respond to it.

Here are some tips that helped me take action in the face of fear.

- **Recognize fear as an emotion but not necessarily a negative one.** Many of us associate fear with negativity, viewing it as something so daunting that we might want to hide from it or deny its presence. However, the first step to confronting it is acknowledging its existence. Reflect on how you feel when fear strikes and how you typically relate to this emotion. Ask yourself, *What do I tell myself when I'm scared? How do I usually respond* (fight, flight, freeze, or fawn)*? What is fear actually trying to communicate to me?*

- **Sit with the fear as long as you can until you're ready to address it.** While writing this book, I subconsciously just wanted to close my laptop, get in my car, and run away from the fear. But I committed to sitting with the fear and observing what arose. This isn't an easy practice, so if you struggle with it, consider asking a coach to help you navigate through your emotions and understand yourself better. The more you sit with the fear, the less imposing it becomes, and the more control you begin to feel over it.
- Once you're able to sit with the fear and understand what's triggering it, **start replacing your fears with affirmations** that help you take steps toward doing it anyway. Here are some of the affirmations I found myself writing:

  - You are strong.
  - You are unstoppable.
  - You rise stronger than you've fallen.
  - You are a force to be reckoned with.
  - You are capable of going through your emotions and letting go of anything that's not serving you.
  - You are loved just the way you are.
  - You are not perfect and that's okay.

- Just do it. You'll thank yourself later.
- Feel the fear and do it anyway.
- Don't believe everything you tell yourself!

If you find yourself holding back because of certain beliefs you have about yourself, I suggest doing the following exercise.

When you have taken the time to list all your dreams, even before using the THAT Framework to set your plan on achieving (later in the book), write a list of what you believe is holding you back from achieving those dreams.

After that, ask yourself, and be honest, *If I wasn't afraid of anything, what would I do?*

When you know what you would do, reflect to discover what's holding you back. Is it anything you listed above, or is it just you and the thoughts you've put in your head?

If it turns out to be YOU, then let's do this! Write down the belief that's limiting you from pursuing your dreams, then try re-writing it so it supports you in being who you need to be to achieve your dreams. For example:

Limiting belief: *I don't think I can achieve my dreams because no one from my family has made it, so why would I?*

Replacement: *I can achieve my dreams. No one has made it in my family, but that doesn't mean I can't. I can and I will!*

Once you've written out your new beliefs, keep repeating them until you start living them. All you need to do is create a habit of believing in yourself until you truly believe in yourself.

If you simply don't understand where your fears are coming from, I recommend seeking help from a coach who will support you in better understanding yourself and becoming aware of the experiences within your mind, heart, and body. All these aspects are linked and interwoven to help you grasp your whole true self.

Remember, each voice in your head represents a different facet of who you are. In the end, your task is to discern how they serve and support you in becoming the best version of yourself, creating an optimal blend of your true self, your THAT.

Chapter 10:
Don't Numb Your Feelings, Write About Them!

One of the biggest struggles I've faced is learning how to express my feelings, because I was taught to suppress them my whole life. I was brought up in an environment where silence was the solution to balance the anger and temper of others. I was constantly told that I was to be quiet and not talk back or defend myself so others wouldn't get mad. I was told to silence my own emotions and not share them so peace and harmony would fill the place. And because of that I grew up afraid of confrontation, expressing my emotions, and setting boundaries to my own feelings and space. Perhaps you relate to one of these situations too. Either you were shamed for the emotions you feel and worry you will be looked down on when you share them, or you grew up with the belief that expressing how you feel is considered talking back and disrespectful, and you need to maintain peace in the household. All of these are ways we are taught to numb our feelings. For me, that resulted in numbing my emotions through eating. I headed to food for comfort and to feel safe. Food was a way for me to focus on something without thinking or expressing. It became an unconscious habit, and consequently I have been obese for a very long time. The main emotion I wasn't able to express was anger, and that came from all the different beliefs I grew up with in relation to my role as a daughter and woman in the household.

I lived a big portion of my life not crying; not a single tear would come from my eyes. Even when I was angry, I would just go silent and ignore everyone. If I was happy, I rarely shared that emotion either. I lived a very long time thinking that was normal and that crying is a sign of weakness. If that isn't numbing my feelings, I don't know what is. The hardest transition I had to make was to confront all the emotions I had suppressed for years, and that eventually translated into physical pain. I've struggled with shoulder pain for a long time, as well as lower back pain and an upset stomach. I had a large cyst on my ovaries, which required surgery, when I was just seventeen years old. And I suffered from obesity as well.

I wanted to keep a journal, like many other girls, but whenever I opened a notebook to start writing, I'd just stare at the blank page for a while and then close it, never returning to it. This happened so many times I stopped keeping count. I loved writing stories and poems, but when it came to what I was experiencing or how I was feeling, that block was persistent.

It wasn't until I turned twenty-six years old that I started to write a blog about my life. I was so afraid of people knowing how I felt about things, I kept it anonymous and never told anyone about it. Once I got into coaching, I truly had to face myself. I began writing about everything going on in my head: how I was feeling, why I felt that way, what I was telling myself, how I spoke to myself, and how much of it was true.

At first, I would just write a few words that summarized how I felt, but the more it became a habit, the more I would write, until I got to a point where I was writing nonstop. My writing was filled with tears, anger, and happiness all mixed together.

Here were the piled-up emotions I was finally able to express to myself. It was just me vs. me. It felt so liberating because I could finally understand what I was going through. It felt like I had opened a faucet and now I couldn't close it until everything inside was let out!

Because I'd been shamed and silenced for expressing how I felt and what I went through, I had to relearn what it meant to feel and to let go of the fear of confrontation. Confronting meant I needed to express my feelings, but there was still a limiting belief inside me shaming me whenever I wanted to. To this day I'm genuinely putting in the effort to let it go and replace it with a belief that helps me grow stronger and stronger, and boy have I made a difference in how I confront people now.

So, rather than numbing your emotions and hiding them away, write about them. Just like I'm writing about mine in this book. Even though sometimes I feel vulnerable and exposed when I revisit my writing, I remind myself that through this sharing and writing, we not only find ourselves but also connect with others on a deeper level.

If you've been shamed or silenced for sharing your feelings, or grew up suppressing them, this is your sign to start writing. I'll share some steps on how to get started, especially if you've never written about your feelings before.

But first, here's how writing and expressing your emotions on paper can help you.

- It will give you clarity on what's really going on in your head.
- You'll learn to understand yourself before you react. In other words, writing can be a proactive way to understand your triggers.
- It will help you make better decisions, because rather than you speaking or reacting out of an imbalance of emotions, you'll be able to center yourself and then make a decision with clarity, confidence, and conviction.

Here's how can you start writing.

- Don't judge yourself on what you write or how you write it. Remember, this is a mechanism to help you understand yourself, and a support tool for you to develop and improve as a person.
- Give yourself permission to write as much or as little as you need each day.
- Never let the pen or pencil leave the paper. Each time you finish a sentence, keep the pen touching the paper so that subconsciously you're preparing your brain to release more writing that needs to be done. You'll find the words flowing out of your mind.
- Don't feel like you have to go back and read what you've written, especially if it's coming from emotions such as anger. In this case, going back and reading it can take you to a place of judging yourself and what you're thinking of, which can restrict you from writing more in the future. If you're writing a hate letter or expressing your angry emotions, I would suggest you write every single thought that comes to your mind. Even if it comes out as scribbles, let it all out, and then tear the paper up and throw it away!

Chapter 11:
The Hidden Messages in Life's Moments

I often felt as though I was drifting through chapters of my own story, surrounded by moments, people, and experiences that I struggled to make sense of. There were times when rejection or judgment weighed so heavily on me I couldn't understand why these experiences were happening. But over time, I realized they weren't just random occurrences. They were teaching me lessons, preparing me to face what was coming next. Life's challenges weren't meant to break me but to build me, guiding me closer to my true THAT.

How many times have we encountered people who left us with a big question mark about why they were in our life? How many times have we been rejected for something we wanted desperately or found ourselves wondering why we go through certain hardships? These questions aren't just rhetorical, they're invitations from life and God to dig deeper, to reflect, to understand the hints that are guiding us in directions we might not immediately comprehend, but that are crucial for the next phases of our journey—guiding us toward our THAT, our true purpose, our true self.

My own life is a testament to these hidden messages. Some of the lessons I've learned, I've shared earlier in this book, but the one that stands out most to me is the feeling of rejection—particularly rejection based on appearance, something I've struggled with so much when it comes to my weight. In many cultures, including Middle Eastern societies, women are often confined to rigid norms of what they need to be or look like to be considered suitable for marriage or even considered beautiful.

I remember vividly the times I was refused for something as superficial as my appearance. I was judged not for who I am as a person, not for my character or my spirit, but because I didn't fit into society's mold of what a woman should look like. One moment that stands out was when I faced rejection from a couple of suitors for marriage simply because of my weight. It crushed me, leaving me with a feeling of unworthiness that lingered for months, if not years. But as time passed, I began to look back on that experience and see it differently. That rejection wasn't a reflection of my value—it was a reflection of their narrow view of beauty. I had to learn that those judgments were opportunities for me to break free from the need for external validation. Instead of letting those rejections tear me down, I started to use them as fuel to build myself up.

Standards of beauty and acceptability are so ingrained in our societies that we often don't question them. But when you're on the harsh receiving end of such judgments, it's not just a cultural norm, it's a personal wound that keeps reopening if the root of the cause isn't healed. How many women have lost confidence because of comments they've heard about their appearance?

You're too fat. You're too skinny. Muscles are for men. You're tall. You're short. Your nose is big. Your cheeks are big. You need

Botox. Your skin is sagging. You need a tummy tuck. You need to stop eating. You have stretchmarks. You have acne...

And although social media today promotes body positivity, it still upholds certain ideals of perfection. Beauty still has rigid standards. For a long time, I allowed these societal pressures to define my self-worth. I believed that if I didn't fit into these categories, I wasn't good enough. But slowly, I began to realize that these painful experiences—whether it was rejection for not fitting into a societal standard or derogatory comments about my appearance—were happening for a reason.

The message I kept missing wasn't that I wasn't good enough but that I needed to stop allowing external judgments to define me. Each hurtful remark was an opportunity to learn something new about myself: that I was strong, resilient, and worthy of love as I was. It wasn't easy, but every time I felt like I was being broken down, I slowly began to change my mindset and use those same experiences to build myself up.

I've always questioned who exactly sets these standards of beauty when, in the Quran, Allah says, (20:4) "لقد خلقنا الانسان في احسن تقويم" which translates to, "We have certainly created man in the best of stature." If God has created us in the best form, who are we to say otherwise? Yet, every time I faced a comment about my appearance, I came to believe there was a hidden message behind this challenge. It's a message that will keep returning in different forms until I stop, listen, and learn from it. For me, the reason this message kept returning was because I needed to learn how to love myself as I am, despite the standards of beauty society had drilled into me. I needed to accept myself the way I am and love every part of me to truly internalize that lesson. And once I learned this, people's judgments stopped being triggers. In fact, they became arrows of love that I now take with a whole heart, increasing my love for myself and my self-worth. Reminding myself of my worth simply from being created in this world, and having that reassurance from the words of Allah, built a momentum of self-love and a desire to be better for myself—not for others.

I realized through reflection and my deepening faith that each of these painful experiences was, in fact, a gift. They were signs from God, urging me to look inward and redefine how I viewed myself. The Quranic verse, "We have certainly created man in the best of stature," became a personal mantra. I would remind myself of these words every time a negative thought crept in, every time I felt inadequate. And I consciously chose to see each moment of pain as an opportunity for growth rather than a moment of defeat. My faith taught me that hardship was a bridge to ease, and the more I embraced this, the more resilient I became.

Life is like a book, filled with chapters waiting to be read and understood. Each chapter, whether it brings joy or challenge, carries a message meant to guide us on our journey. It's like a gentle whisper in our ear, nudging us toward growth, understanding, and self-awareness.

But how do we untangle these messages? How do we learn to listen to what life is trying to tell us and what God is trying to show us? The process is both simple and profound. It begins with pausing, reflecting, and truly listening to our hearts. In those quiet moments of contemplation, when we strip away the noise of the world, we can begin to understand what our journey is trying to communicate to us.

Difficult experiences often carry with them lessons of patience and resilience. A chance encounter with a stranger might remind us of the beauty and importance of human connection. Even setbacks, as painful as they may be, can serve as steppingstones to something greater. As the saying goes, "When one door closes, another door opens." This idea is beautifully echoed in the Quran, where we are reminded, "إن مع العسر يسرا"(94:6) , "With hardship comes ease."

These hidden messages are not just lessons for the present, they're also guidance for the future. By learning from our past experiences, we equip ourselves with the wisdom and strength needed to face whatever lies ahead. We become more resilient, more insightful, and better prepared for the adventures and challenges yet to come.

I've come to see every hardship, every moment of rejection, as a step toward something greater. When I finally learned how to listen to these hidden messages—messages that were urging me to love myself as I am—I was able to transform my pain into power. The judgments that once tore me down now serve as reminders of how far I've come. I no longer shy away from life's challenges. I confront them head-on, knowing that they are steppingstones toward becoming the best version of myself, the closest version to my true THAT.

So, as you continue your journey, remember to look for the hidden messages. They're there, waiting for you to discover them. And as you do, you'll find that life's challenges are not obstacles but steppingstones on your own path to becoming your most authentic self. Most importantly, learn how to confront these lessons, not shy away from them. That's how you will grow into the better version of yourself, fueled by your experiences rather than torn down by them. Each lesson, whether wrapped in hardship or disguised as a challenge, is a part of your journey toward your true THAT.

Chapter 12:
The Foundation for Transforming Your Life: Believing in Yourself

Believing in yourself is more than just a motivational phrase. It is the cornerstone of achieving your dreams and living a fulfilling life. This mindset empowers you to face challenges, seize opportunities, and embrace your unique journey with confidence. Have you ever sat down and asked yourself, *Do I truly believe I have what it takes to achieve my dreams?* If you have, what was your answer? What was the conversation that followed?

If the first voice you heard in response was one of doubt and disbelief, then it's time to take action and change the narrative you have about yourself. The conversations you have inside your head can either make you or break you. They are the foundation upon which you build your self-worth, your confidence, and your capacity to achieve your goals.

As a woman, I often catch myself grappling with imposter syndrome. Trust me, it's something I've been working on for years, and it still pops up from time to time, especially when new challenges and bigger dreams come into play. However,

I'm aware of it, and I don't let it take over my worth or belief in myself. Imposter syndrome, or the persistent doubt in one's own abilities despite evidence of success, is a common experience that can undermine self-belief, particularly in women.[3]

Self-worth is crucial when it comes to reclaiming your THAT—your true self. Losing it means that somewhere along the way, you lost your love for yourself, your trust in your abilities, and your confidence in who you are. Many women lose confidence in how they look after gaining a few pounds or having babies. Others lose trust in themselves because of mistakes they made in the past and still regret. Some women live their entire lives without understanding their worth because they were never taught to put themselves first or to show up for themselves every day.

Recently, I saw a reel on Instagram about how women in the workforce have been breaking barriers and shattering glass ceilings in demanding what they deserve and fighting to have their voices heard. But when it comes to their personal lives, many still lack the confidence to believe in themselves, especially when it comes to communicating their needs. This is heartbreaking because it shows that, despite all the progress, there's still a long way to go in reclaiming our THAT—our worth, our confidence, our courage, and our true selves fully in all aspects in life.

You might ask, "Why is it so important to believe in myself?" Let me break it down for you. Imagine you're on a journey, and

---

[3] Clance, P. R., & Imes, S. A. (1978). *The Impostor Phenomenon in High Achieving Women: Dynamics and Therapeutic Intervention. Psychotherapy: Theory, Research & Practice*, 15(3), 241–247. Available at: <u>American Psychological Association</u>

you can see your destination in the distance. You're ready to embark on this journey, but you don't have all the tools and equipment you need at point A to get to point B. Those tools are your self-worth and how much you believe in yourself. Without them, you'll find it difficult to move forward and reach your destination.

Self-belief is the foundation upon which all success is built. Without it, even the most talented and capable individuals can find themselves paralyzed by doubt and fear. When you believe in yourself, you tap into an inner power, strength, and resilience that propels you forward, no matter the obstacles.

Self-belief...

- **unlocks your potential.** Self-belief allows you to recognize and unleash your full potential. It encourages you to take risks, try new things, and push beyond your comfort zone. It's what helps you think outside the box about what you need to reach your destination of self-love and reclaim your THAT.
- **builds resilience.** Believing in yourself fosters resilience. When you trust in your abilities, setbacks become temporary challenges rather than insurmountable barriers. Resilience is crucial in helping you understand when to keep moving and pushing, even when you feel like giving up on yourself and your dreams.
- **cultivates a positive mindset.** Self-belief nurtures a positive mindset, which is essential for maintaining motivation and enthusiasm, especially during difficult times. We truly know our strength during challenging moments, and equipping

ourselves with a positive mindset helps us overcome them and move forward with clarity and vision.

Now that you understand the importance of believing in yourself and regaining control over who you are, let's explore how self-belief can transform your life. I'll start by sharing a personal story about how it changed my life.

In 2019, when I first began my coaching journey, I had a vision of building a community of women in Qatar who support one another, openly discuss the challenges we face as women, and share a space where we could learn from each other and grow together. At that time, there wasn't a community like that around me, but I was determined to create one. I didn't know if I would find people who resonated with this vision, so I took it to social media and invited women to come together for open discussions on topics that I felt would resonate, especially within our society. I was hesitant at first because it was something new and untested. But if it wasn't for my belief in myself and the value of the work I do, I wouldn't have taken the leap and started this community. This community is called *You're Not Alone*, a community from women to women. It started with monthly gatherings discussing topics related to women such as imposter syndrome, fear, relationships, work life balance. But now, five years in and counting, I have built a community with over one hundred members who I am incredibly proud of and who have become part of the beautiful change we see in our society. Through our different activities and events they have found themselves, learned to love themselves, and accept themselves in a very safe space. They inspire me every day to continue doing what I do.

This is just one example of how believing in yourself can profoundly transform your life. Here are a few other ways self-belief can impact different areas of your life:

Career

Self-belief can lead to career advancement and fulfillment. When you trust in your abilities, you're more likely to take on challenging projects, seek promotions, and pursue your career aspirations with determination. There have been so many barriers broken by female leaders who inspire us to show up for ourselves and demand what we deserve in recognition, positions, and a seat at the table. Don't let societal talk about women "not being able to have it all" or being judged based on personal factors such as marital status or motherhood, hold you back. Your skills, abilities, and dedication are what should be judged, not your personal life. The more you believe in yourself, the closer you'll get to achieving your career goals.

Relationships

Confidence in yourself enhances your relationships. It allows you to communicate more effectively, set healthy boundaries, and attract positive, supportive people into your life. Your confidence reflects your presence and authority over your life, influencing how others treat you. Recall the times when you were confident in yourself. How did that change the way others perceived and treated you? Now think about how that differed when you showed up with less confidence. Recognizing the power you have as a woman is crucial, as we are natural leaders, even in relationships. Though it may not seem obvious from the outside, women often orchestrate everything from behind the scenes. To be THAT woman, you need to believe in yourself and the value you bring to the world.

Personal Growth

Self-belief encourages continuous personal growth. It motivates you to pursue lifelong learning, develop new skills, and constantly strive to become the best version of yourself. When you believe in yourself, you believe that you deserve better, and this belief fuels your desire to grow and improve—not for others, but for yourself. The joy of reflecting on your growth, whether over the past month or the past year, is unparalleled. Personal growth allows you to look at life through a positive lens and gives you hope to do more and be more. I always say that life ends when you stop learning and growing, not when you actually die. So, see how you can live fully each day and believe that you are worthy of a fulfilling life.

Well-being

A strong sense of self-belief contributes to overall well-being. It reduces stress, anxiety, and self-doubt, promoting a healthier, more balanced life. In today's fast-paced world, where we are constantly glued to our phones and laptops, it's easy to get distracted and overwhelmed. My relationship with my mobile devices has become an addiction that I work on daily to break free from. The notifications, the endless scrolling, the subconscious comparisons to others' lives—these are stressors that have increased chronic stress and depression, particularly among younger generations. We focus so much on the outer world that we neglect our inner world, which is key to maintaining our overall well-being. Let go of the external stressors that make you doubt yourself and focus on nurturing your inner world.[4]

As you move on to the next part of the book, remember that believing in yourself is not just a nice-to-have, it's *essential* for achieving your goals and living a fulfilling life. It's time to take action—reclaim your THAT, embrace your self-worth, and let your belief in yourself propel you to new heights. As you transition into the next section of this book, which focuses on the 20 percent action needed to achieve your dreams, keep this truth in mind: Self-belief is the foundation upon which all success is built. Equip yourself with the tools of self-worth, confidence, and resilience, and watch as your dreams become your reality.

---

[4] Sorenson, S., & Garman, K. (2013). *How to Prevent Burnout: Engage Employees and Reduce Stress in the Workplace.* *Gallup

PART 2:
Taking Action!

Chapter 13:
Stop Complaining About Your Life and Start Doing Something About It!

Let's start taking action! We're not playing any games, we're not fluffing the words to make you feel better, because we're all about being true to ourselves, pushing ourselves to be the best versions we can be, and reconnecting to our THAT.

It's always surprising how many people I come across who complain constantly about their life. Nothing is working out for them, or they don't have the money to travel or start a business, or they're in a bad relationship, or they're being abused one way or another, or that they're not healthy, or that they're struggling to achieve their dreams, or they don't have time for themselves... If I had a dollar for each complaint I've heard, I promise you I would be a millionaire by now.

But what frustrates me the most is how people find it so easy to complain and so hard to do something about it. Whenever I come across someone who is constantly complaining, my first question becomes, "And what are you doing about it?" Once I start dropping this question on them, be it friends, family, or even clients, I can see the silence in their eyes and the setback they get, especially when they least expect it.

Maybe that sentence was a bit triggering for you, especially if you tend to feel as though you don't have control over the circumstances in your life. But hear me out in this chapter, and I'm confident you'll find some inspiration and some answers to what you're going through.

There are two types of people in this world: those who complain for the sake of complaining, with no intention to become better or do better; and those who complain but realize it's *them* stopping themselves, so they start doing something about it.

Would you believe me if I told you at some point in my life, I was the first kind?

Yeah, it's hilarious, especially now that I'm a coach pushing people to achieve their goals and live their lives with purpose and meaning. Ironic, I know! But in some way, I guess it was meant to be, because if I didn't know how it felt, I don't think I would be able to help people the way I do today, pushing them beyond the complaining stage that gets them nowhere and helping them set a plan to achieve the life they want.

Sometimes we find ourselves trapped within our minds because of what we've been through, or who we believe we are, and the longer we've lived that way, the harder it is to escape or the more daunting it seems, because fear of the unknown and the change that comes with it plays with our head and thoughts. We convince ourselves we're not allowed to dream outside of the box. We think it might be bad or a sin to dream big, dream different, or just be different.

I struggled with this battle inside me for years. Part of me had big dreams and wanted nothing more than to chase them and achieve them and truly believe that the sky is the limit, but then the other part of me would do anything to silence that voice, to be "normal" and "fit in" so I would be accepted, loved, and appreciated by others.

A lot of factors added to this struggle. Being in a big family where each one of us was fighting to be seen and loved by our parents was one. I come from a big family, which is typical for Arab families and typical in the Gulf especially, so I'm sure a lot of you will relate to this part of the story. I was one of seven siblings, and one of the middle children, and I have been told before that I do give off a vibe of a middle child...

I truly believe that each sibling got a different version of our parents. I even see that when my siblings and I share stories of our childhood and how our parents treated us. But it takes some great awareness to realize this and truly accept your parents for who they are and what they have done for you, because deep down they have done the best they could within the circumstances they had. It does take a lot of courage to let go of the grudges we hold against them, but we need to let go of them to be able to move on and do the best we can for ourselves and for future generations.

As a child you crave your parents' attention, because they are the first two people you see in your life and they automatically become the people you want to love, have, and hold on to for the rest of your life. But in a big family not only does that love become divided, you sometimes might also not get everything you need due to circumstances out of your control. How do we cope with not always getting what we need? Some people might act out and be loud (these are people who are always fighting and shouting to seek attention). Others become quiet and obedient (because they believe that listening and doing everything your parents ask of you will get you their love and attention and recognition). Others might become perfectionists due to conditional love given to them while young, whereas yet others become high achievers because they got recognition and love only when they achieved things. I became the quiet, obedient, perfectionist middle child who just wanted to please her parents for their attention and love. Think about how all these situations start creating so many beliefs about ourselves. And all these beliefs are set in stone in our mind during the first six to ten years of our lives.

But then you're faced with a choice: Do you want to live your whole life working toward getting your parents' love and attention, or do you want to take on the harsh reality of learning how to get for yourself what you weren't able to get from your parents?

I also struggled with the fact that I grew up in two different countries. I was born in Qatar but moved to the US with my family as an infant and stayed until I was nine years old, before we returned to Qatar for good. Being brought up one way and then have that shift upon moving to another country really affected me. It was a huge cultural clash, which was really hard to deal with as a nine-year-old. It's difficult for a kid to go through all that when they are still figuring out who they are and who they want to be. So, I found myself both fighting to fit in and yearning to break free and just fly!

But over time I've learned that everything takes time, and I *will* get to where I want to be once I learned to stop complaining and started taking action on what I can do and provide for myself and for others around me. But for me to do that, I just have to 1) be patient, and 2) be willing to put in the effort to work toward the life I want. This is what DOING means.

Your dreams won't all come true at once, but the small steps that you take every day—even though you'll often think they're not enough—are what will get you to the success you aspire to. It's shifting from a complaining scarcity mindset to an abundant positive mindset that will help you do that.

Here are some tips for you to STOP doing at this moment and tips to DO at this moment!

Tips to STOP

- **Stop** victimizing yourself and *start* taking responsibility and control of your life.
- **Stop** focusing on what you can't control. You can't control others, but you can control yourself; you can't control your family, but you can control your interactions with them; you can't control what others think about you, but you can control what you let affect you or what you believe about yourself or how you react...
- **Stop** thinking that you don't have a choice, because even not choosing is also choosing.
- **Stop** being overly independent, and start asking for help when you need it. We all have our blind spots, so asking for help from trustworthy people or professional people can lead to a major mindset shift.

Tips to DO

- **Do** write down what you would want to achieve if you weren't afraid of anything in the world.

- **Do** find your "why"—the reason you do what you do, or what we call your purpose or calling in this world. It will make all the efforts you put toward achieving your dreams worth the work.
- **Do** prioritize yourself, as no one will come to save you! **You** are responsible for your life and actions, no matter how great the support you get from the people around you. **At the end of the day, it's you against you, and not the world.**
- **Do** learn how to love yourself, because this is key to start doing—the fact that you believe you DESERVE a better life!

We explored previously how important it is to take care of yourself before you take care of others, because filling your cup and watering your own garden will give you the opportunity to grow and heal and support others. It doesn't work the other way round. One of the most important steps to start taking care of yourself is to stop complaining and start taking action toward a better life and a better THAT. It's about moving from a complaining mentality to an action-based mentality.

One of the most beautiful success stories I had with one of my clients was when they were able to change their relationship with their mother. Their relationship with their mother was so draining and affected their self-confidence. This showed in how everything they accomplished was to get the validation they had been looking for their whole life. They were always complaining about the need to get that validation, to stay small, to not shine their light because they wanted to be accepted by their mother. We looked at how they might find that validation within themselves, and their whole world shifted. And the biggest win was how their love for themselves and their self-confidence has rubbed off on their family, and especially their mother. My client became a great example for their family, which changed the family. That's called the ripple effect.

I will share some exercises I do with my clients that creates this shift in mindset, because creating that shift will truly get you the results you want. You just need to put in the work.

Exercise 1: **Identifying Complaints and Victim Mentality**

The objective of this exercise is to help you recognize your recurring complaints and determine if you have a victim mentality.

Instructions

1. List your complaints

Take a sheet of paper and divide it into two columns.

In the left column, write down all the things you frequently complain about in your daily life, whether it's about family expectations, social norms, work, or any other area.

2. Analyze your complaints

For each complaint, ask yourself the following questions and write your answers in the right column.
- Why does this bother me?
- How often do I complain about this?
- Do I feel powerless or like a victim in this situation? Why?

3. Reflect

Review your answers and identify any patterns. Are there recurring themes where you feel like a victim or where you see yourself as powerless?

Example

Complaint	Analysis
My family expects me to follow certain traditions that I don't agree with.	I feel restricted and frustrated. I complain about this daily. I feel like a victim because I believe I have no choice and must abide by their rules.

4. Discussion

Reflect on how often you complain and whether these complaints are connected to a victim mentality.

Discuss how recognizing these patterns can help you take control of your mindset. Take the time here to reflect within your journal or notebook, to understand your thoughts. Once you understand where these complaints are coming from, it's time to take some action and shift your mindset.

Exercise 2: Transforming Complaints into Action Points

The objective of this second exercise is to shift from a complaining mindset to an action-oriented mindset by focusing on what can be controlled and making actionable plans.

Instructions

1. Revisit your complaints
Take the list of complaints from Exercise 1.

2. Identify control and influence
For each complaint, ask yourself these questions.
- What aspects of this situation can I control?
- What aspects are beyond my control?

3. Create action points
In a new column, write actionable steps you can take for the aspects you can control.

For the aspects you cannot control, write down how you can change your perspective or response to the situation.

4. Prioritize and plan
Prioritize the actionable steps based on their impact and feasibility.

Create a timeline or plan to start implementing these steps.

Example

Complaint	Control	Action Points
My family expects me to follow certain traditions that I don't agree with.	I **can** control how I communicate my feelings, set boundaries, find compromises. I **cannot** control my family's beliefs or their insistence on traditions.	1. Have a respectful conversation with my family about my feelings and perspectives. 2. Seek a middle ground or compromises that respect both my individuality and family traditions. 3. Establish personal boundaries and find supportive networks or mentors who understand my situation.

5. Discussion

Reflect on how taking action on what you can control empowers you and reduces feelings of helplessness. Write down how you will feel when you take this action, what results you will get, and how that will support you. Also write down what that would look like, feel like, sound like for you, and how this will serve you in the long run (five, ten, thirty years from now).

After deciding your action steps, take one complaint and start implementing the action steps by setting a plan for what you promise yourself you will do, how often you will do it, and what that will give you.

Example: I promise myself to vocalize my opinion in a respective way when my mother brings up the subject again. I will give her space and listen to what she says rather than being defensive and just wanting to reply. I will practice active listening more on a day-to-day basis. When I apply this, it will give me calmness, it will give me more power over myself, and give me the confidence to be who I am without disrespecting or belittling others.

These exercises aim to foster a proactive and empowered mindset, helping you take responsibility for your life and make positive changes.

A SUCCESS STORY:
Transforming Complaints into Action

One of my clients (let's call her Amira) was caught in a toxic cycle of seeking validation from her narcissistic father. Every achievement she made was in the hopes of getting his love and recognition, but she always felt empty because her achievements were measured by how much attention she would get from her father. It never worked. She constantly complained about how her father's expectations were holding her back from being herself and that her self-worth was based on what he thought, but she wasn't doing anything to change it.

Through our sessions, we shifted her focus. Instead of seeking validation from others, we worked on finding that validation within herself. Over time, not only did her relationship with her father improve, but she became an example of self-confidence and strength for her entire family. The ripple effect of their transformation changed the entire dynamic at home. That's the power of action!

Next Steps: Let's Take Action!

If you want to change your life, you need to stop complaining about what's wrong and start doing something about it. Use the exercises and tips above to help you shift your mindset and take real, actionable steps toward the life you deserve. Each small action builds momentum, and before you know it, you'll find yourself closer to your THAT than you ever imagined.

Remember, your future self will thank you for starting today!

Chapter 14:
I'm So Many Things, Why Do I Need to Choose One?

One of the most inspiring videos I've ever seen was a TED Talk by Emilie Wapnick called "Why some of us don't have one true calling." I was in awe of the whole talk because it spoke to a side of me that I hadn't been able to comprehend, let alone explain to others, which was that I felt I didn't have one true calling. Emilie referred to these people as "multipotentialites." A multipotentialite is a person who has more than one potential or area they can be great at.

The idea of an Arab woman having multiple callings is rarely encouraged. The message I often heard growing up—and one that still echoes for many women around me—was to pursue education not as a means to change the world but to have it as a backup plan. A degree, no matter how valuable, was to be kept discreetly in the background, like an insurance policy for when life didn't go as planned, specifically when marriage wasn't the expected outcome. Ambition, for many, was something to be downplayed, and standing out wasn't always celebrated. The focus was more on securing a stable future, often shaped by societal pressures to marry and settle down rather than carving a path toward personal greatness.

In our community, women are often encouraged to earn their degrees but not necessarily to push boundaries or make significant waves in the professional world. Instead, they are told to achieve just enough to stay prepared for life's uncertainties but not to pursue their callings with full force. The concept of success is often linked to safety, not transformation. This idea leaves many feeling boxed in, holding on to passions they may never fully explore because they've been conditioned to prioritize stability over daring to dream.

Have you ever lived your life being asked to choose one thing you're good at and be that? Or when you were little, were you always asked what you wanted to be when you grew up, and you don't even remember what you wanted to be or you always had a problem choosing just one thing?

The other day, I asked my niece what she wanted to be when she grew up. You know what she replied? She said, "I want to be a doctor, a firefighter, and a teacher." I almost challenged her on that. I admit, I was coming from a mindset that she needed to pick one thing and let that become her destiny. Ironic, since I'm a multipotentialite person myself. It's so funny how the expectations we experience as kids can stick with us. I immediately encouraged her to not choose but rather explore and see where she finds herself.

I remember seeing videos of parents in certain cultures and traditions getting their months-old children to choose a profession by crawling to the object that represented that profession, and that then would become their career and destiny. Other cultures and traditions don't allow women even to choose, because their future was already decided for them. Sometimes the expectation is just to grow up to be wed and start bearing the children of the next generation, without looking at the person's dreams of doing something for herself.

What are we doing when we squish the next generation into the molds that have held us back from becoming multipotentialites, from spreading our wings to be all that we want to be? We've seen what it's done to us and how it's held us back from doing the things we love and are pretty good at. We've seen how, because of that, we've lived in fear of straying from the norm. We've seen how many people, because of that, will hide certain aspects of themselves, or even worse, bury them and never think about them again. I've had so many people tell me how much they miss drawing, writing, singing, or creating art just because it's not what they were "good" at, or because they had to "grow up" and leave those things behind. These things can feed our souls and just make us dance from inside, or even better, zone out and forget about the outer world. Yes, if you haven't noticed yet, I'm a creative at heart and love creating and innovating and just bringing something new to life, something that has my "touch of Asmaa" no matter how big or how small the thing.

That's the beauty of being a blend of different things. You can be great at doing different things, as long they feed into your true purpose in life. That's the difference between your purpose and your callings, or at least that would be how I would define them and differentiate them. You may have one purpose in this world, something so unique to you that no one else is purposed to do it or bring it to the world; what might be called your reason for being born. However, your callings are here to help you fulfill your purpose, which can come through many paths.

I believe one of the most important things is to know your purpose, just as important as knowing your name. And I believe your purpose doesn't change, but your callings to how you carry your purpose throughout can be based on different stages in life.

Let's take me as an example. I came to the conclusion that my purpose is to inspire other people and support them to live a life with purpose. It took me a while to find my purpose because it needed a lot of exploration. I explored what I really enjoyed, what came easy to me, and what I could make a living out of and never get bored of. At first, I thought I had to be a coach. Then I realized I could also inspire people through my creative side and my art. Then I found out I could help others find their purpose through my writing (after all, you're reading this book!) and later I discovered my passion for being a speaker, a businesswoman, and many other roles. All different callings that feed into my purpose in life. And that's when I realized I'm not just destined for one true calling. I'm a multipotentialite and can serve my one purpose in many ways.

You might hear you can only be great at one thing and just be good at other things, which might be the case for some people. It doesn't make them any less or more worthy. You might also want to live a life with one true calling toward your purpose, and that's fine as well, but this chapter is for the people who have felt trapped in the need to choose to be great at only one thing even though they have the potential to be great in many other ways as well.

If you're a multipotentialite, even if you've disconnected from the different sides of yourself and different callings due to societal constraints or any other reason, I would like you to do the following and regain your different callings to your true purpose in life. You might ask, "But what is my purpose?" Or "I haven't even taken the time to understand or know my purpose to know my callings in life." Well, you are in the right place, my dear reader.

Finding your purpose is akin to discovering your THAT. This quest for purpose goes beyond achieving external goals or meeting societal expectations. It's about uncovering the core of your being and understanding the unique value you bring to the world. When you find your THAT, you connect with your deepest desires, passions, and strengths. This connection acts as a compass, guiding you through life's uncertainties and helping you navigate challenges with resilience and clarity. It provides a sense of direction and meaning, transforming your actions into purposeful endeavors that align with your true self. The title of the book is the true essence of what it means to find your purpose in life.

Knowing your purpose, or your THAT, is crucial because it grounds you within your identity. It helps you strip away the layers of societal conditioning, expectations, and roles that often obscure your true self. This process of self-discovery allows you to live authentically, making choices that resonate with your inner values and aspirations.

Moreover, finding your THAT fosters a profound sense of fulfillment and satisfaction. It instills a sense of belonging and significance, reminding you that your existence has a unique purpose. This realization empowers you to pursue your passions and make meaningful contributions to the world, creating a legacy that reflects your true soul.

In essence, discovering your THAT is a journey of self-awareness and alignment. It's about embracing who you are at your core and living in harmony with your inner truth. This alignment brings a sense of peace and contentment, because you no longer strive to fit into molds that don't reflect your true self. Instead, you create a life that is authentically yours, filled with purpose and meaning.

Ultimately, knowing and finding your purpose is about reclaiming your THAT—your unique identity and role in the world. It's a journey of self-empowerment, enabling you to live a life that is true to yourself and impactful to others. By embracing your THAT, you unlock your potential and create a life that is not only fulfilling for you but also inspiring and uplifting for those around you.

The moment I found my purpose, or my THAT, was the exact moment I understood why I do what I do and how everything now falls into place after that. I was fortunate to be able to support so many women find their true purpose, their own version of THAT, and live a life true to their purpose. The most common sentence I hear my clients repeat is that everything now makes sense, and we make sense to ourselves. Decisions are easier to make because they are based on whether they take them closer to their purpose. I always say it's a combination of your purpose and your core values that become the compass that you build your life around. I've had clients finally let go of the inauthentic version of themselves they had created for the sake of others and embrace their true THAT after finding their purpose.

It might seem daunting to let go of that facade you created for a long time and to be someone different, even though it's really just you showing up as your highest true self. I remember that moment very clearly when I let down my own wall and learned how to live a life close to who I am. And because of that, my whole life shifted.

You need to keep holding on to that small ray of hope that one day you will be able to find your THAT. And that's all it takes: hanging on to that hope and continuing to fight for yourself until you find a soul able to understand your THAT and accept you for it. That moment can be with you reading this book. I can see you, I can hear you, and I am there for you. Trust me, if I was able to do it and find myself, my THAT, so can you.

But how can you know your purpose in life?

Finding your purpose begins with understanding your passions, strengths, and values. Here's a simple exercise to guide you through the process.

1. Reflect on your passions
- *What's something you love so much you would do it 24 hours a day if you could?*
- *What could you do even if you weren't paid to do it?*

Write down the activities that bring you joy and fulfillment. These are strong indicators of your purpose.

2. Identify your sources of peace
- *What do you find yourself doing when you want to relax or be at peace?*

Note the activities that provide you comfort and calm. These reflect your true self and align with your purpose.

3. Recognize your strength
- *What's something you're great at and are known for among your family and friends?*

List the skills and talents that others recognize in you. Your natural abilities are often tied to your purpose.

4. Consider your value
- *What's something you can do that people would pay you for?* Think about the skills or services you offer that others find valuable. This helps connect your purpose with potential career paths.

Values Work: Defining Your Core Values
Your core values are the principles that guide your decisions and shape your life. Knowing your values is crucial to living a purpose-driven life.

Instructions for Choosing Core Values
1. **Reflect on your life:** Google "core values" and have a look through the different lists available. Review and think about which values resonate most with your experiences, beliefs, and aspirations.
2. **Prioritize:** Select five values that you feel are most important to you. These will be your guiding principles.
3. **Align actions:** Consider how your daily actions align with these values, and identify any areas where you might need to make changes to live in greater alignment with your core values.

This exercise is a crucial step in understanding your purpose and living a life that is true to who you are at your core.

Putting It All Together: Living a Purposeful Life

Now that you've explored your passions, strengths, and values, it's time to integrate them into your life.

- **Write down your purpose:** Based on your reflections, write a statement that encapsulates your purpose. This could be a simple sentence that reminds you of what you're here to do.
- **Explore your options:** Consider the different ways you can live out your purpose, whether through your career, hobbies, or volunteer work.
- **Embrace multipotentiality:** If you have multiple interests and callings, embrace them! You might find that your purpose is multifaceted and can be expressed in various ways.
- **Trust in your uniqueness:** Remember, your combination of passions, strengths, and values makes you unique. Let that uniqueness guide you toward a life of purpose and fulfillment.

By following these steps, you'll be well on your way to discovering and living a life that is aligned with your true self and core values, bringing you closer to the life you were meant to live.

A SUCCESS STORY:
Knowing your purpose and values gives you clarity

I had a client (let's call her Sarah) who came to me confused, lost, and stuck. She wanted help but whenever I asked her questions to understand what she wanted help with, her answers were always "I don't know." Whenever I asked her about what she was feeling, she would say, "I don't know." Whenever I asked her about what she wanted to achieve, she answered, "I really don't know." I then asked her one more question: "And if you did know, how would your response change?" There was a long pause, and it was that long pause that indicated she was digging deeper into her own thoughts to find the answers. Once she did, she shared that she didn't know because she had never given herself the time to think about what she wanted to achieve. So that is where we started, working on her purpose and core values, so that she knows why she does what she does and how her values play a role in her life. We finished our sessions, and months passed. Then she came back to thank me for the clarity she now has. "Knowing my purpose and values makes everything so easy now! I can say no to what doesn't align with my purpose and values. I now can make faster decisions because I know my inner compass and how to be present with myself and how I feel and think about everything around me, and without you I wouldn't have gained that clarity."

Moments such as those remind me of my own purpose and values as a coach and why I do what I do.

Chapter 15:
Envision It to Achieve It! Vision Boards Really Work!

I never believed vision boards worked until I tried them and began seeing results. Now, I'm their biggest advocate. I've always been a visual person. I remember what things look like, and I can visualize my thoughts. Some might relate (which likely means you're a visual person too), whereas others might not because they could be more audio or aesthetic individuals.

Being a visual person helped me greatly in imagining how I wanted my life to be. As you know, I've always had lots of dreams, and being stubborn works in my favor here—I would do anything to achieve those dreams. Many people have called me a dreamer, but not in a good way, more like in a "you need to be realistic and stop dreaming so big" way. This could be because my dreams scared them, or maybe they had never learned to dream big or understood what dreaming big really means.

However, being a dreamer isn't what got me into vision boards. It was the fact that I had many dreams stuck in my head and, for a while, wasn't doing anything about them. I've always felt like I would be something when I grow up, someone important, successful. I wasn't sure what that was, but I had a spark in me. When I was young, I used to watch Oprah with my mother and dream of having my own successful show that helped people in different ways. When I got older, I dreamt of someone who lived abroad, learning about different cultures and just seeing the world. I dreamt of having my own company that flourished and had branches all over the world, becoming so successful that I could inspire others to do the same.

I always felt that I couldn't play small because that's not who I was. My problem wasn't in the dreaming, it was the fact that I never did anything about those dreams. I was dreaming but not taking action, and it felt frustrating all the time. I had to keep my dreams to myself because people around me didn't truly understand what I wanted, and I was hard on myself because I felt stuck, thinking I had no power to go after my dreams. Can you relate?

We often keep dreams in our heads but don't act on them because we feel we need a full plan before taking the first step. That's the difference between having dreams and achieving them. We all have dreams or goals, but the gap between dreaming and doing is where vision boards can support you.

I started using vision boards just as an experiment to see if they might help me achieve the dreams and wishes I'd stacked up in this little head of mine. I wanted to learn more about the science behind them and how they work. When I delved deeper and started to implement vision boards, I was astonished.

How Vision Boards Work

As humans, we're capable of processing seventy to eighty thousand pieces of information through our brain in seconds! From those thousands, we tend to filter out most and just focus on five to seven pieces of information in a moment. We subconsciously make that choice based on what seems most relevant to us in that moment. For example, imagine there's a car you're dying to buy, and you've set the intention of purchasing it. Suddenly, you start to see this car everywhere on the streets, even in the exact color you want. It's not that everyone suddenly has the car, it's because your mind has tuned in to noticing it. That's exactly how vision boards work.

When we write down or visualize what we want to achieve, we start to filter out everything that isn't serving us and focus on our goals. Anything that reminds us of our dream appears more frequently in our awareness. It's not that opportunities are suddenly more prevalent, but we've programmed our mind to stay focused on them.

Of course, vision boards by themselves don't make things happen; you still need to put in the work. But they support you in keeping your eye on the prize and not letting distractions take away from your energy. Remember, this isn't a magic trick where we visualize our dreams and expect them to manifest without effort. It's a mindset tool that helps you focus on what's crucial for you to achieve and ensures that you live the life you aspire to, rather than one filled with unrealized dreams.

So, when you create your vision board, it's important to put it somewhere you can see it every day. This way, it will subconsciously remind you to set the intention for your dreams and work toward achieving them. The best feeling you can have is when a year or two passes, and you look back at your vision board, realizing you've accomplished what you set your mind to. It's such a beautiful feeling!

Steps to Create Your Own Vision Board

If you haven't tried vision boards before, I hope this chapter inspires you to start. Here's a step-by-step guide to creating your own vision board and what to focus on.

1. Define your goals

Start by getting clear on what you want. Sit in a quiet space and reflect on the different areas of your life: personal, professional, financial, and spiritual/emotional. Write down your goals in these categories, even the ones that seem out of reach. Dream big and be honest about what you want.

2. Gather your materials

You can create a physical board (poster, corkboard, etc.) or a digital board using apps such as Canva or Pinterest. For a physical board, gather magazines, scissors, glue, and markers. For digital, find images and words online that resonate with your vision.

3. Visualize your future

Imagine what your life would look like once you've achieved your goals. How would you feel? What would your daily routine look like? The clearer you can picture it, the better. It would be great to give your visionboard a theme or title as well, and that becomes the center.

4. Select your images and words

Find images, quotes, and affirmations that represent your dreams. These can include
- **Images:** pictures of the lifestyle you desire, places you want to visit, and relationships you want to nurture

- **Words:** inspirational phrases, affirmations, or powerful words such as "Growth," "Love," or "Abundance"
- **Feelings:** visuals that evoke the feelings you want to experience, whether it's confidence, joy, or peace

5. Arrange and create your board

Once you've gathered everything, start placing the images and words on your board. You can group them by themes or mix them together, whatever feels right to you. This is your vision, so it should reflect what resonates most deeply with you.

6. Place it where you can see it

Place your vision board somewhere you'll see it every day, for example, your bedroom, office, or bathroom mirror. For a digital board, make it your phone or laptop wallpaper.

7. Take action

Remember, vision boards don't work without action. The more you act on your dreams, the more aligned opportunities will appear. Start by taking small steps toward your goals every day.

Focus Points

Clarity: Be clear about what you want and make sure your vision board reflects that.
Consistency: Look at your vision board regularly to keep your goals at the forefront.
Belief: Believe in your ability to achieve your dreams.
Action: Vision boards are powerful, but they require you to take action in the real world.

Creating vision boards has transformed my life, and they can do the same for you. My first vision board was created as part of my professional coach training, where at the end of the course, we were to visualize our success and what it meant for us. I remember clearly that board, which included: owning a house (which I do now *Elhamdellah*), a plane that signified wanting to travel more (which I have), the love of my family always around me and supporting me in whatever path I take (I am so grateful to their support within this journey), me smiling while holding my own book, with a standing ovation from the audience for the upcoming book launch (which I am working toward as I write this book) and my book as a *New York Times* Best Seller (which hasn't happened yet but setting the intention for it to happen!), and a picture of me and my small family (which hasn't happened yet either). Looking back at this first vision board, I am so proud of the number of dreams I was able to turn into my own reality!

Whether you want to focus on your personal life, career, or even spiritual growth, vision boards can help you stay focused on your goals and turn your dreams into reality, and don't forget that the way to your THAT can also be done through a vision board.

So, what are you waiting for? Start your vision board journey today and watch your dreams unfold!

Chapter 16:
Setting Intentions and an Action Plan Is a Game-changer

Have you ever found yourself doing something, knowing in your mind that it won't work, worrying about how badly it will go, or how frustrated you are about doing it, and then in the end, it turns out exactly as you imagined?

Now remember a time when you set your intention that it would turn out better than you expected, and you truly felt you would get what you needed; the yes you were looking for, the thing you dreaded saying coming out smoothly, the conversation you were afraid to have turning out to be one of the best you've had. Or maybe you found the dress you were looking for, aced the interview, and landed your dream job?

I've been through each of these scenarios so many times. I remember bringing up the topic of me wanting to travel abroad to study for my master's degree. I was deeply terrified and felt that my father would say no. And that was the exact answer I heard. On the other hand, I remember how confident I was about getting a corporate client for a training, going into the interview clear about what I bring to the table and the value I add, and thinking that whatever happens is going to happen, all I am responsible for is how to be the best version of me and showcase my value. Every time I asked myself why I can predict or always feel inside what will happen, do you know what I discovered? It's because of the intention I set subconsciously before doing what I do.

We often underestimate the power of intention-setting, even though, for Muslims, it's a significant part of our religion. We're rewarded based on the intention we set, "و على نياتكم ترزقون".

Some of us have been doing this our whole lives without knowing it. What we want to start practicing is setting intentions *intentionally*, with awareness. This itself will become a game-changer for you in who you are, what you become, and what you achieve.

We all have dreams we hope to reach one day, right? But as days go by, that "one day" seems more distant. We find ourselves immersed in the *later, not now, it's impossible, I can't, I'm too old, I'm too young* mentality. Some of us live so much in our heads that we talk ourselves out of doing things rather than taking action. This can result in not taking steps toward our dreams, not taking risks, not confronting someone about issues, or not doing something out of our comfort zone. This is often because of that voice in our head, that voice that can hold us back from so much more, the same voice that will keep using worst-case rather than best-case scenarios.

But the more we're in our heads, the more we lean toward setting the wrong intentions. What does that mean? Setting intentions consciously for everything we do, even day-to-day tasks such as driving the car, starting the day, praying, getting dressed, going to work, or whatever it may be, helps us adopt a positive mindset. When we set the intention that today is going to be a great day and then let it be, 99 percent of the time, the day will be great! When we set the intention of wanting God to answer our prayers visibly, 100 percent of the time they will be, and you'll see the result right in front of you, no matter how long it takes! Setting your intention for anything and letting it be is essentially the meaning of what we call in Islam *Tawakkul*, where you decide in your heart how you're going to approach a situation, wanting what's best in the end, and trusting that you will get there with God's grace.

Our job in this world isn't to know how things are going to get done; that isn't within our control. What we can control is the intention we set for ourselves when we're doing something, no matter what that thing is. *Tawakkul* is genuinely believing deep down that things will work out the way you hope, and then just letting them be!

I've seen the differences between approaching tasks with a positive intention and mindset versus a negative one. And I continually remind myself why it's important to set the right intention when doing anything during the day.

We've heard so much about the idea that "you are what you think," or "you attract the thoughts that are in your head." This is precisely what setting intentions means.

When we begin practicing a positive mindset toward everything we do and set the intention to do our best and get the result we hope for, that positivity becomes what we attract.

So, what are some ways you can support yourself in building your positive mindset and setting positive intentions?

- **Practice affirmations.** Your affirmations are your intentions. If you go into a job interview feeling as though you're not good enough for the job, you've already set yourself up for failure. Deep in your mind you've started to look for all the signs that you're unworthy, then boom: you likely won't get the job! How about flipping this scenario by setting the intention that you *will* get the job because you're qualified, capable, worthy, and they need you more than you need them? See how things change as a result of that intention, and trust that if you haven't, there's something so much better coming your way.
- **Remember that whatever doesn't happen for you just wasn't meant for you; it was a lesson you needed to learn.** Having that positive mindset will help you move past what you might see as failures and prevent you spiraling into negative thoughts such as *I'm not worthy, I'm the problem, I'm the issue, I'm a failure*, etc. I always believe that everything happens for a reason, and every incident is already a win-win situation, because either you will get what you want, or you will learn a valuable lesson you needed to learn that will prepare you for what's coming for you.
- **Start setting positive intentions with awareness!** You can remind yourself to do this by writing your intentions on pieces of paper you place around your room, a reminder on your phone, or even changing your phone's wallpaper. The more you practice, the more it becomes a habit.
- **Don't forget to focus on what you can control.** You can set the intention and let go of what you can't control, such

as the outcome, the timing, or the method. Those things are left to the creator of creations. Submitting to that fact helps you avoid overthinking and allows you to live in contentedness.

So, start every day by voicing your intention aloud, and see the positive impact it has on you and your life. This technique can calm your nervous system, especially if you're an overthinker like me. It helps you live in the moment and not dwell on the future. It's a learning process, but once you get the hang of it, it can work wonders.

Crafting your Personal Action Plan

For you to craft your journey back to your THAT, you need to first understand where you stand. Navigating your current situation is one of the first things I would do with you if you worked with me as a coach. We call this the Current Situation Assessment. Here, you will find eight different steps that you can do to assess your current situation. You will find that after doing all these steps you will have so much more awareness regarding what you need to focus on and what action you need to take in order to become a better version of yourself.

1. Circle of life mapping
Objective
Reflect on your current life circle and identify key areas of focus.

Instructions
Draw a circle, then divide it into segments representing key areas of your life: Family, Career, Health, Social Life, Personal

Growth, Spirituality, and Community Involvement. This is what we call in coaching the Circle of Life.

Rate each area from 0 to 10 (0 being the lowest and 10 being the highest) and draw a line that represents where you are in the area. Reflect on each segment and write down what actions you need to take, if any, to reach your desired score.

2. Reflection session
Objective
Create a space for self-reflection and honest assessment.

Instructions
Set aside quiet time for reflection, away from distractions.

Write a dialogue between your current self and your future self, discussing your current situation and what you need to do to take responsibility and improve your circumstances. Speak to yourself as if you have already achieved your dreams and goals, and now you are looking back to your current self with advice on how to get to where you need to be. This dialogue will help you immerse yourself with being and feeling your best version, and identifying what it takes to be just that.

3. Commitment plan
Objective
Commit to actionable steps to take responsibility for your life.

Instructions
List specific actions you will take to improve each area of your life based on your circle of life and action plan.

Visualize your progress as you follow through on your commitments, and set realistic timelines for each action. Make sure that your goals are SMART (Specific, Measurable, Achievable, Relevant, and Time Based)

Chapter 17:
Self-Care Strategies for Busy Lives

Do you know that the first thing that's usually neglected by women juggling their multiple roles is self-care? It's the first thing that goes out of the window when women feel they don't have time to finish their tasks as employees, mothers, wives, etc. However, creating and applying self-care strategies is *crucial* for maintaining a harmonized and fulfilling life. These strategies act as a foundation for managing stress, improving mental health, and enhancing your overall well-being. By integrating unique and meaningful self-care practices into daily, weekly, and monthly routines, busy women can ensure they are not only surviving but thriving. We want to go from a chaotic mind to abundance in life.

Implementing self-care strategies helps foster a better relationship with yourself by promoting self-awareness, self-compassion, and personal growth. When women take intentional steps to care for their physical, emotional, and mental health, they develop a deeper understanding and appreciation of their own needs and boundaries. This, in turn, empowers them to make decisions that align with their values and goals, reducing feelings of overwhelm and burnout. Ultimately, consistent self-care leads to a more resilient and empowered self, enabling women to navigate their various roles with confidence and grace while maintaining a strong sense of self-worth and fulfillment. The practices in this chapter provide a structured approach to prioritizing personal needs, making it easier to stay connected with yourself despite the demands of everyday life, and truly get you back to your THAT. These are daily practices that I personally incorporate within my own busy life. Juggling a full-time job, a full-on coaching business and community, along with my other roles can be a bit chaotic, and these practices have helped keep me sane. I sometimes feel overwhelmed or on the verge of burnout, but these practices help me become aware of what is truly happening in my mind and support me in what I am capable of. It helps supplement the support I also get from my accountability partners and my own coach (yes, every coach needs a coach). You don't have to incorporate all of them at once, but see which resonate with you. Remember, it's about consistency rather than aiming for perfection. With practice, they'll become easy to incorporate into your daily routine.

Daily Practices

1. Micro-meditation moments
Practice: Integrate one- to two-minute micro-meditation moments throughout your day. These can be within your daily prayer practice, to sit for one or two minutes after each prayer to just breathe and be present with yourself, make *dua*, or even set your intentions and just breathe.

Importance: These short, intentional pauses help you recenter, reduce stress, and improve focus without taking much time. They have supported me in emphasizing *Tawakkul* on Allah for the coming future.

2. Personal check-in

Practice: Set a daily reminder to ask yourself, *How am I feeling right now?* and *What do I need at this moment?*

Importance: This encourages self-awareness and helps you address your needs before they escalate into stress or anxiety. These questions are like a reminder to yourself to be present with yourself.

3. Empowered decision-making

Practice: When faced with a decision, pause and ask, *Is this decision aligned with my values and purpose?*

Importance: This practice ensures your actions are purposeful and aligned with your long-term vision, fostering a sense of control. This specifically has helped me make faster decisions on what to do and what not to do. Doing things that are truly aligned with your purpose, values, and goals in life can be a game-changer.

4. Intentional moments of joy

Practice: Identify and engage in small activities that bring you joy, even if it's just for a few minutes, such as listening to your favorite book or savoring a cup of tea.

Importance: Regularly experiencing joy boosts your mood and reminds you of the pleasures in life, helping you stay connected to what matters. You deserve to be happy, and these moments produce endorphins that can support you with your everyday tasks. You can always face life with a more positive mindset.

Weekly Practices

1. Scheduled "me time"

Practice: Block out at least one hour a week for yourself to do whatever you enjoy without any interruptions.
Importance: Having dedicated time for yourself helps you recharge and reinforces the importance of self-priority. This can be a solo date in your favorite café to read your favorite book, or that weekly massage that helps you destress, or an outing with close friends who make you forget that time exists when you're with them.

2. Personal growth check-in

Practice: Reflect on your personal and professional growth over the week. Identify one thing you learned and one area you want to improve.
Importance: Regular reflection keeps you aware of your progress and areas for growth, maintaining a forward momentum.

3. Purposeful connections

Practice: Reach out to a friend, coach, or mentor for a meaningful conversation that inspires or supports your growth journey.
Importance: Deep, purposeful connections provide emotional support and perspective, crucial for maintaining balance in a busy life. These conversations are another level when they are with someone who will support your growth and your mindset. These kinds of conversation fuel and inspire me, giving me a

bigger overlook on what I'm doing, and how I can incorporate this new learning to my journey to be closer to my THAT.

Monthly Practices

1. Value alignment review
Practice: Once a month, review your values and assess if your daily actions align with them. Adjust where necessary. These can come from the list provided in the previous chapter.
Importance: Ensuring your actions align with your values fosters a sense of integrity and purpose, reducing internal conflicts and supporting clarity on what you want out of life.

2. Vision board update
Practice: Spend time updating or creating a vision board that reflects your goals and dreams. Place it somewhere visible.
Importance: A vision board keeps your goals in sight and motivates you to take consistent actions toward achieving them.

3. Self-compassion ritual
Practice: Create a ritual that celebrates your achievements and shows kindness to yourself, such as writing a letter of appreciation to yourself or treating yourself to something special.
Importance: Regularly practicing self-compassion reduces self-criticism and enhances your resilience and well-being. Remember to always prioritize yourself within your schedule. When you feel the need to scratch one thing to have a shorter to-do list, remind yourself over and over again, *Taking care of myself is a priority, I will not be able to do the other tasks if I scratch the most important task I have on that day.*

One practice I cannot emphasize enough is: _____

Practicing Stillness

It's crucial to learn how to rest without feeling guilty. Practicing stillness and resting is as important as any achievement you accomplish. Staying still and resting can be a hard task, especially for those of you who are overthinkers. This section will guide you through practical steps and insights to help you embrace a stillness mindset, ensuring you can find peace and tranquility amid the hustle and bustle of your daily life.

The Power of Saying No

One of the most effective ways to create space for stillness is by learning to say no. This can be challenging, especially if you are used to prioritizing others' needs over your own. However, saying no is not about being selfish but about setting healthy boundaries to protect your time and energy.

- **Assess your commitments:** Regularly review your commitments and obligations. Identify tasks or activities that are draining your energy and do not align with your goals or values.
- **Prioritize:** Focus on what truly matters to you. By saying no to less important tasks, you free up time for rest and activities that rejuvenate you.
- **Practice polite declining:** Develop polite ways to decline requests. For example, "I appreciate the offer, but I need to prioritize my current commitments," or "I'm unable to take this on right now, but thank you for thinking of me."

Cultivating Patience

Patience is a crucial element in embracing a stillness mindset. In a world that often values speed and efficiency, developing patience can help you appreciate the process rather than just the outcome. I always thought I was a patient person, but chasing my dreams and achieving really taught me the importance of patience, along with *Tawakkul* to keep me having faith in God and myself to achieve what I aspired to achieve. Here are some tips to support you with cultivating patience.

- **Mindful waiting** Use moments of waiting (in lines, at traffic lights) as opportunities to practice patience and mindfulness. Focus on your breath and observe your surroundings without judgment.
- **Embrace imperfection** Understand that growth and progress take time. Embrace the journey, including its setbacks and challenges, as essential parts of your development.
- **Slow down** Intentionally slow down your pace in daily activities. Whether eating, walking, working, or cleaning, take your time to savor the experience and stay present.

Finding Joy in Stillness

Discovering joy in moments of stillness can transform how you perceive rest. Instead of viewing stillness as unproductive, recognize it as a valuable and fulfilling part of your life. This is vital for those who would stress about stillness and not doing anything. I have had clients who resist stillness and rest because they are afraid of the negative inner voice that can eat them up if they don't give it anything to keep it busy. But these moments of stillness help silence the inner critic and pump up the volume on our true self, the leader within, to find joy within the stillness.

- **Create rituals** Establish daily or weekly rituals you look forward to, such as a morning meditation, a quiet cup of tea, or an evening walk. These rituals can become cherished moments of stillness.
- **Engage in hobbies** Pursue hobbies that bring you joy and allow you to lose track of time. Whether it's reading, gardening, or painting, engaging in activities you love can create a sense of stillness and fulfillment.
- **Connect with nature** Spend time in nature to find stillness and joy. Whether it's a walk in the park, a day by the sea, or simply sitting in your garden, nature has a way of grounding us and bringing peace.

And sometimes you don't want to do anything and that is okay!

I was coming back from my Eid travels, where I had totally disconnected to be present with myself—not thinking about work, clients, emails, what I had to do when I got home—and I didn't want to do anything when I landed. And by anything, I mean literally I would lie down and do nothing for days. I didn't want to think about work, clients, emails, or my to-do list, because I felt like doing *nothing*.

There was a time when I would beat myself up whenever I was doing nothing. I viewed my worth through the lens of accomplishments: the busier and more accomplished I was, the more value I gave myself. When I had nothing to do, I felt as though I was wasting my life, not working toward my goals. Do you know how I would get myself back to work? By comparing myself with others. I would tell myself that if I kept slacking off, I would be a nobody, that I would get left behind. For a long time, whenever I took a break, no matter how badly I needed and deserved it, I would beat myself up over doing nothing.

Can you relate? If you can, know that you've been conditioned to believe that your worth is tied to how much you've accomplished. Yep, that's a limiting belief there for you. It took me a while to find this pattern, even though I'd believed it since I was a little kid. This belief becomes a nightmare if you grow up wanting to be something. People who become workaholics or feel as though they can't sit alone by themselves and do nothing, people who are always looking for the next big thing to accomplish, people who never celebrate their successes—these are the people in whom you'll most likely find this limiting belief engraved.

The funny thing is that even after months of working with my own coach on this limiting belief, sometimes I still find myself falling back to it. I won't lie and say that I was able to completely eliminate this limiting belief from my head, but now I am able to recognize it and flip the belief immediately. Most important, I've learned how to silence that critic voice that's feeding it. (Side note: This is why we as coaches work on giving you the tools to be able to recognize when you fall into a habit or a subconscious thought, and how to support yourself to get through it, because that's how growth happens.)

This same limiting belief even surfaced when writing this chapter. I've gone back and forth trying to finish it, but for some reason it doesn't want to get written. This is the longest I've spent on a chapter. Every day, I open my laptop to start writing, I just look at the screen, then I close it. I open it again to motivate myself to start writing, but nothing. I actually go to my mobile phone and start procrastinating! Yes, procrastination comes crawling into this scenario too, accompanied by the limiting belief and bringing back the perfectionist mentality.

Even worse, I start to question whether I'll ever finish this book. So instead of doing something about it on the spot, instead of confronting all the doubts, I tend to numb the feeling by procrastinating. Then I become aware of the procrastination, become aware that what I'm doing is giving myself permission to believe all these untrue thoughts. I remind myself to sit in the feeling of discomfort, to understand why I'm telling myself these words and doubting myself and my worth. I write down how I'm feeling (writing is therapy), and when I start to see the pattern clearly, I begin to replace it with the truth: *Just let it flow and it'll come out like it needs to. Being perfect is a myth. Just do the best you can with what you can and the resources you have. Remember why you wanted to write this book; it's because you wanted to help others like you to understand themselves and process what needs processing so they can get out of the loop of doubt and start believing in themselves.*

I know what you're thinking: *But you're a coach. You should have already worked on yourself. How can you help other people if you're still going through those same struggles?* Yes, I'm a coach, and trust me, I've worked on myself and will keep on working on myself, but it's a life journey of growth. I can never stop working on myself because every day I discover things about myself. It can be new information, new experiences, new emotions; whatever it is, my work is to be aware of what I go through and give myself the space to process it all and keep showing up for myself. That's how I become better, by letting go of old habits and building new ones that support me becoming a better version of myself every single day.

So, if you feel like you're not worthy, take a break from your busy days and just breathe. Try processing that emotion and build a new belief about your worth, one that's unrelated to your accomplishments.

Being busy all the time is not healthy for you, physically or mentally. We're human and we need to take a break once in a while. If you find yourself heading to burnout, here are some tips to help you take care of yourself.

Tips for Not Doing Anything

- **Social media breaks** Cut off your social media access as it's a key driver of stress. It easily leads to comparing yourself to others, their journey, or their content. Whatever it is, take that social media break and it will help you so much with your self-worth.
- **Mental days off** If you're heading toward a breakdown at work, take a couple of days off for yourself. They're worth it. Spend time with yourself and with people you love, doing things you love and disconnecting from the world a bit. And if you have more time and have the money, book that flight and spoil yourself with a trip. Traveling feeds the soul.
- **Work out for your mental health** I've found working out and finding something I enjoy doing have helped a lot with my stress with work and with having a busy schedule. I try to devote forty-five minutes to an hour, three or four days a week, to disconnect and focus on my workout. Every time I finish, I feel ten times better than when I started. Even if I don't feel like it, I still force myself to work out, because it really helps me stay sane as a busy woman who's always on the go.

- **Write what you go through to build internal awareness**
  You will never regret writing down your thoughts and feelings and decompressing your mind. And if you don't have that capacity and need help, don't be afraid to ask for it. Reach out to friends or specialists within the field you need help with, whomever you need to support you.

A SUCCESS STORY:
The Art of doing LESS!

I gave a motivational speech to the Chapter of Certified Accountants in Qatar about the art of doing less. The room was filled with men and women who strive to be the best, as becoming a chartered accountant is not an easy certification to attain. These were busy people who barely have time for such speeches yet found the time to be part of this event to network with other chartered accountants. Listening to my speech was a bonus, I guess! I remember taking them through an exercise of how they can shift the focus back to themselves, stop thinking for a bit, and just do less. It was such a simple exercise, yet the feedback I got after that talk was phenomenal. People were thanking me for what I supported them to do. I had participants say they'd never been able to silence their mind before doing this exercise. Others were saying how that moment had given them inner peace and Zen. And this was just for five minutes. So, imagine doing it as a daily or weekly practice, and think about how truly it can affect your work and level of energy.

Chapter 18:
Balancing Stability and Passion

In the pursuit of our dreams, it's easy to get swept up in the excitement and emotional pull of passion. For many, this might mean making significant decisions—such as quitting a stable job or entering a marriage—based purely on our heart. Although passion is an essential driver of fulfillment and success, stability provides the necessary foundation to sustain those dreams. This chapter provides a structured game plan to help you balance stability and passion, ensuring that your decisions are both emotionally satisfying and logically sound.

As someone who built most of my decisions on how I felt, I needed to bring my rational voice into the mix to make sure I had the right balance when it comes to making decisions. Yes, your sixth sense is important and gives you an indication about certain situations, but sometimes we can let our emotional mind override our rational voice. Sometimes the right decision doesn't feel good, but it's still the right decision. That is why understanding the balance between both and operating from a place of both passion and stability will be such a powerful tool to add to your repertoire.

Understanding the Balance

Balancing stability and passion means harmonizing your heart's desires with your mind's rationality. This balance is crucial for sustainable success and long-term happiness. Without stability, passionate pursuits can lead to stress and regret. Without passion, stability can lead to stagnation and unfulfilled potential. The goal is to find a sweet spot where both elements coexist, empowering you to pursue your dreams confidently and responsibly.

The Game Plan: Balancing Stability and Passion

1. Self-assessment: know your true self

- **Identify core values** Reflect on your core values and what truly matters to you. Understanding your values will help you make decisions that align with both your heart and mind.
- **Evaluate current situation** Assess your current job, lifestyle, and financial stability. Identify which aspects of your life provide stability and which areas you are passionate about.
- **Define your passion** Clearly articulate what your passion is and why it matters to you. Understanding the depth of your passion is crucial for planning.

2. Set clear, realistic goals using the THAT framework

The THAT Framework is a unique goal-setting approach I created. It is designed to help individuals achieve their goals while aligning with their identity, values, and purpose. The framework includes distinct elements related to self-discovery and actionable steps that differentiate it from other models such as SMART goals.

Here's an overview of the THAT Framework.

T: True Alignment
- Focus on setting goals that are deeply aligned with your core values, beliefs, and purpose.
- Ask: *Does this goal reflect who I truly am and what I truly want?*

H: Holistic Growth
- Ensure the goal supports growth in multiple areas of your life (personal, professional, emotional, spiritual).
- Ask: *How does achieving this goal impact other parts of my life positively?*

A: Actionable Steps
- Break the goal into specific, manageable actions that can be executed realistically.
- Ask: *What small steps can I take today to move closer to achieving this goal?*

T: Transformational Impact
- Evaluate how achieving the goal will transform your life or the lives of others.
- Ask: *What long-term change will this goal bring to my life, community, or world?*

How is this framework different from other frameworks?
- It's self-centered (in a positive sense) in that it encourages individuals to connect with their authentic self while pursuing goals.
- It focuses on long-term transformation rather than just ticking off tasks on a day-to-day basis.
- It considers the broader life context of goals, including cultural and societal influences.

3. Create a transition plan
- **Financial planning** Build a financial safety net. Save a percentage of your income to support yourself during the transition. Consider creating a detailed budget that accounts for both current expenses and future needs.
- **Skill development** Identify any skills or knowledge gaps that need to be addressed to pursue your passion. Invest in training, education, or experiences that will equip you for success.
- **Timeline** Establish a realistic timeline for your transition. Set milestones that mark significant progress toward integrating your passion into your stable life.

4. Test the waters
- **Part-time pursuit** Start working on your passion project part-time while maintaining your current job. This allows you to gauge its viability without sacrificing stability. Many successful businesswomen manage to balance their full-time job with their passion projects, gradually building their passion into a sustainable career.

- **Pilot projects** Launch small-scale projects or services related to your passion to test the market and refine your approach based on feedback.

5. When to keep both and when to choose one
- **Assess work-life balance** If your full-time job and passion project both bring you joy and you can manage them without getting overwhelmed, it's possible to maintain both. This dual approach can provide financial stability while allowing you to pursue your passion.
- **Signs to choose one** If your passion project starts generating enough income and you find it more fulfilling than your full-time job, it may be time to transition fully. Similarly, if managing both leads to burnout or negatively impacts your health and well-being, consider choosing the one that aligns more closely with your long-term goals and values.
- **Decision criteria** Evaluate the growth potential, financial implications, and personal fulfillment of each option. Consult your support network and mentors to gain different perspectives before making a final decision.

6. Seek support and mentorship
- **Find a mentor** Seek guidance from someone who has successfully balanced stability and passion in their career. Learn from their experiences and advice.
- **Build a support network** Surround yourself with supportive friends, family, and professional contacts who can provide encouragement and practical assistance.

7. Evaluate and reflect

- **Regular check-ins** Schedule regular check-ins with yourself to evaluate your progress, reflect on challenges, and celebrate successes. Adjust your plans as needed.
- **Emotional and practical balance** Continuously strive to maintain a balance between emotional fulfillment and practical considerations. Be mindful of emotional impulses and ensure they are balanced with rational planning.

8. Making the leap

- **Readiness assessment** Before making any significant changes, assess your readiness. Consider factors such as financial stability, market readiness, and personal well-being.
- **Confident transition** When you feel confident that you have a solid foundation and a clear plan, make the transition. Trust that your preparation and planning will support your success.

Balancing stability and passion is not about choosing one over the other. It's about integrating both to create a fulfilling and sustainable life. By following this game plan and utilizing the THAT Framework, you can make informed and balanced decisions that honor both your heart and mind. Whether pursuing a new career, starting a business, or making significant life changes, this balanced approach ensures that your passion is supported by a stable foundation, leading to long-term success and happiness.

Making Conscious Choices

How can you tell if the decision you're making is conscious or subconscious? Within the awareness section, we discussed that not choosing is, in fact, still making a choice—often an unconscious one. This can be particularly detrimental when you're on the journey to reclaiming your true THAT and showing up fully for yourself.

In this section, I will guide you on how to make conscious decisions, whether they are quick, on-the-spot choices or long-term decisions that will significantly impact your life. Making conscious decisions means being fully aware of your choices and their consequences, ensuring they align with your true self and long-term goals. On the other hand, unconscious decisions are often reactive and may lead to outcomes that don't serve your best interests or reflect your values. The exercises and processes outlined here will help you identify whether your decisions are conscious and guide you toward making more deliberate and thoughtful choices.

Exercise: Identifying Conscious and Unconscious Choices

1. Reflect on Recent Decisions
- **List recent decisions** Write down five to ten recent decisions you've made in various areas of your life (e.g., work, relationships, personal growth).
- **Describe each decision** For each decision, describe the process you went through. Did you pause to reflect? Did you gather information and consider options?

2. Analyze Your Decision-Making Process
- **Conscious vs. unconscious** Identify which decisions were made consciously (with awareness and deliberation) and which were made unconsciously (habitually or impulsively).
- **Criteria for analysis**
  - Did you align the decision with your core values?
  - Did you consider the long-term consequences?
  - Did you seek information and different perspectives?
  - Did you balance emotions with rational thinking?

3. Reflect on Outcomes
- **Positive outcomes** Note the outcomes of the decisions you identified as conscious. How did they benefit you or align with your goals?
- **Negative outcomes** Note the outcomes of the decisions you identified as unconscious. How did they detract from your goals or values?

4. Develop a Conscious Decision–Making Plan
- **Set intentions** Commit to making more conscious choices. Write down your intention to pause, reflect, and align decisions with your values.
- **Create reminders** Use reminders (sticky notes, phone alerts) to prompt you to pause and reflect before making decisions.
- **Practice mindfulness** Incorporate daily mindfulness practices to enhance overall awareness and presence.

5. **Practice and Reflect Regularly**
- **Daily practice** Start each day with a brief mindfulness session and a review of your core values and goals.
- **Evening reflection** End each day by reflecting on the decisions you made. Were they conscious? What can you improve?
- **Weekly review** Set aside time each week to review your decision-making process, reflect on outcomes, and adjust your approach as needed.

Process Template for Immediate Decisions

1. **Pause and breathe** Take a deep breath and center yourself.
2. **Identify the decision** Clearly state what decision needs to be made.
3. **Check core values** Quickly review your core values. Does this decision align with them?
4. **Gather key information** What essential information do you need to make this decision?
5. **Weigh options** Briefly consider the pros and cons of each option.
6. **Emotional check-in** How do you feel about each option? Balance this with rational thought.
7. **Make the decision** Choose the option that best aligns with your values and goals.
8. **Reflect briefly** After making the decision, take a moment to reflect on how it went.

Process Template for Long-Term Decisions

1. **Define the decision** Clearly articulate the decision to be made.

2. **Reflect on core values and goals** Ensure the decision aligns with your core values and long-term goals.
3. **Gather comprehensive information**
   - Research all relevant aspects of the decision.
   - Seek input from diverse sources and perspectives.
4. **Evaluate options thoroughly**
   - List all possible options.
   - Consider the short-term and long-term consequences of each option.
5. **Emotional and rational balance**
   - Acknowledge your emotional responses.
   - Balance emotions with a thorough rational analysis.
6. **Consult your support network**
   - Discuss your options with trusted friends, mentors, or colleagues.
   - Gather insights and advice from different perspectives.
7. **Make the decision**
   - Choose the option that aligns best with your values, goals, and gathered information.
   - Develop an action plan to implement the decision.
8. **Reflect and adjust**
   - Regularly review the outcomes of your decision.
   - Make necessary adjustments based on reflection and feedback.

By following this process and using the templates for immediate and long-term decisions, you can ensure that your choices are conscious and aligned with your true self. This approach not only enhances your decision-making skills but also helps you live a more intentional and fulfilling life.

Chapter 19: Building a Support Network

I created the *You're Not Alone* community because I know how helpful it is to surround yourself with the right kind of support system. It's so crucial for us women to surround ourselves with people who share the same values, who lift us up, and who become our accountability partners. We do come from a collectivistic society, but rather than confining ourselves to the society we are born into, we can create the network we want to belong to, hence *You're Not Alone*. You are more than welcome to join our community, no matter where you are around the world. More on this at the back of the book.

Here are a few reviews some of these amazing women have shared with me about being part of the *You're Not Alone* community:

"You have not only made me become more confident as an individual, but I can also see that reflected within my kids when they see me stronger despite all the difficult times I've been through. They are stronger because I am stronger. Thank you for providing us such a platform to take our time to heal and become stronger, and I really hope my daughter grows to be just like you!"

"You have no idea how much you have touched us and inspired us to be better versions. We have booked each Wednesday for two hours so that we don't have anything booked at the same time as the gatherings of this community. We always look forward to every gathering, sharing and learning from other women."

"I was distant for a while with all the things that brought joy in me because I wasn't motivated to do so for a very long time, and one of those was not having it in me to pick up my business again or do anything towards it because I didn't want to fail. And now I have finally found my purpose again in my business and I was able to pick things back up, and I have you to thank for this. I actually enjoy running my business and I'm not afraid to fail or try new things."

Choosing the Right People for Your Support Network

In a world where culture and tradition often feel like the backdrop of every decision, especially for women in collectivistic societies, having a strong support network isn't just beneficial—it's essential. These networks provide emotional, psychological, and practical support that goes beyond companionship. They become lifelines, offering reassurance and strength through every twist and turn. For many, these relationships are a buffer against the weight of expectations, a source of understanding that resonates with shared cultural values, and a space to navigate the challenges of juggling various roles.

Rebuilding a connection with oneself often requires breaking away from traditional norms, which can be daunting. But when surrounded by the right people—family, friends, mentors, peers—women can step into their potential without fear of judgment. A supportive network can serve as both a foundation and a springboard, encouraging personal growth and enriching one's journey toward self-awareness and fulfillment.

The key to building such a network? Choose wisely and intentionally. Seek relationships that align with your values and offer a sense of mutual respect. Support is most powerful when it's reciprocal, creating a dynamic where growth and empowerment flow both ways.

Not everyone deserves a place in your support circle. When building a network, you want people who will encourage, uplift, and respect your journey. Here are some key types of individuals to consider.

- **Family members** Some family members provide a deeply rooted understanding of who you are and where you come from. Choose the ones who genuinely support your goals and well-being. And remember, for those who may not align with your values, it's okay to set boundaries.
- **Close friends** Real friends are your chosen family. Seek those who encourage growth, honesty, and empathy. They are the ones who provide a safe space for you to share your triumphs and challenges alike.
- **Mentors and coaches** Mentors and coaches with a genuine interest in your development provide guidance and inspiration, helping you reach both personal and professional goals.
- **Professional networks** Surround yourself with individuals who understand the landscape of your field. Professional networks offer career insights, resources, and connections that support your long-term ambitions.

- **Community groups** Engage in local groups that align with your passions, hobbies, or cultural values. These groups can offer not just friendship but also a renewed sense of purpose.
- **Online communities** In today's world, online spaces can be a source of powerful, flexible support. For those who may lack local resources, these communities offer connection anytime, anywhere.
- **Healthcare and wellness professionals** Doctors, therapists, and coaches address not only physical health but also mental and emotional well-being, creating a solid foundation for holistic wellness.

Building a Balanced Support Network

Creating a balanced support network is a process, one that evolves as you do. Here are some steps to help you get there.

1. **Identify your needs** Think deeply about which areas in your life need the most support. Identify the qualities you want in a supportive relationship.
2. **Reach out and engage** Be proactive in building your network. Join groups, attend events, and engage with others who align with your journey.
3. **Nurture relationships** Once you have a network in place, take time to invest in it. Building and maintaining relationships is a two-way street.
4. **Evaluate and adjust** Relationships change, and that's okay. Regularly assess your network and make adjustments to ensure that it remains supportive and relevant.

With a thoughtfully chosen and nurtured support network, women can create a strong foundation that enhances both their inner growth and their outer journey.

Why Meeting New People is Vital for Your Mental Health

Meeting new people isn't just a social act, it's an investment in your mental and emotional well-being. Each connection we make has the potential to become a thread in the fabric of our lives, reinforcing our resilience and helping us feel anchored. Relationships, even casual ones, act as a signal, lifting us up in times of need and reminding us that we're not alone. Every person we meet brings with them a new perspective, a different lens through which to view ourselves and the world.

Through relationships, we rediscover ourselves, often in ways we didn't anticipate. We see our strengths reflected in others' eyes and appreciate qualities we might otherwise overlook. Each connection serves as a mirror, reflecting our value and our potential, showing us that we are not only capable but also that we are enough.

The Growth Connection

Socializing with new people opens doors to personal growth. Every interaction is an opportunity to learn something new about the world, and maybe even more important, about ourselves. Different backgrounds, experiences, and perspectives challenge our beliefs, push our boundaries, and make us more compassionate. These relationships shape us, pushing us to grow into more empathetic and self-aware individuals.

The idea of meeting new people may be daunting, especially for those who are naturally introverted, but it's worth every moment of discomfort. Let me share an experience that changed my perspective on this. In May 2023, I attended the Forbes Women Middle East summit, a space filled with accomplished women, yet I felt out of place. However, each conversation I had was a reminder of my worth and my purpose. Surrounded by inspiring women, I felt empowered to step into my full potential.

On a practical level, our social circles encourage us to stay engaged, motivated, and healthy. Often, good friends challenge us to try new activities, adopt healthier habits, or simply get out of the house. And this gentle nudge toward balance can be one of the greatest gifts of friendship.

A SUCCESS STORY:
A Client's Journey to Fulfillment

I want to share the story of a client who, like so many of us, didn't realize the power of a support network until she experienced it firsthand. Let's call her Layla. Layla was an incredibly dedicated professional, pouring herself into her work, yet she often felt isolated and burned out. As a single mother, her life was a cycle of responsibilities, and the idea of asking for help felt vulnerable and intimidating. She feared judgment, feared opening up to others, and had built walls around herself to manage everything alone.

But eventually, the weight of isolation became too heavy. She decided to attend a local networking event on a whim for You're Not Alone, hoping for a break from her routine. At first, she was reluctant, standing on the sidelines and feeling as though she didn't belong. But little by little, she began to connect with others. She met women who shared her struggles, her dreams, and her values. These weren't just casual encounters. These women became lifelines, forming a circle of support that allowed her to grow and heal.

Through her new network, Layla began to rediscover herself. She started to see her own strength reflected in the eyes of the women around her, and her confidence soared. She learned to embrace her vulnerability, to open up without fear, and to celebrate her journey both as a mother and a professional. With the support of her newfound connections, Layla eventually launched her own business, one that aligned with her passions and allowed her to support other women going through similar journeys.

Chapter 20:
Practicing Self-Kindness

I vividly recall a session we held for my *You're Not Alone* community, during which we explored the theme of transitioning from self-criticism to self-compassion—a journey toward self-love. That session remains fixed in my memory because of the profound impact it had on everyone present. The healing journey is incredibly powerful because it's about mending your relationship with yourself, which is often the most challenging yet transformational process you can undertake.

Practicing self-kindness is essential as you reconnect with your THAT because, along the way, you'll encounter various stages of self-awareness. It's crucial to be gentle with yourself, especially when you confront the darker aspects of who you are, parts you've avoided because of the pain associated with them. To reach the light at the end of the tunnel, you must first navigate through the darkness, and the key to supporting yourself on this path is learning how to practice self-kindness.

At one point during that session one of the members asked, "Why is it so easy to be harsh on ourselves and so difficult to show ourselves love and compassion?" My response was that it's often because we don't recognize our own worth due to the limiting beliefs ingrained in us from a young age, for example, things like, "Don't be arrogant, always be humble," or "Stay like the rest. You're not better than anyone else." These messages get internalized, leading us to constantly question our actions, making sure we fit into the mold of what we're "allowed" to be.

Another reason could be that many of us grew up in environments where criticism was a constant. Over time, the voices of those who criticized us become internalized, turning into our own self-critical voice. This voice often resurfaces whenever we encounter triggers that bring up memories of criticism, pulling us back into those painful experiences.

However, to heal and quiet that critical voice, we must first learn how to silence it and amplify the voice of compassion within us. In this chapter, we'll explore practical ways to practice self-kindness and embrace yourself with compassion, even when you're navigating the darkest parts of your journey back to your THAT.

Transforming the Inner Critic

Objective: To help individuals recognize, understand, and transform their inner critic into a supportive voice, fostering self-love and compassion.

Duration: 20–30 minutes

Materials Needed
- Journal or notebook
- Pen or pencil
- A quiet, comfortable space

Instructions

1. **Set the scene**
   - Find a quiet place where you can sit comfortably and won't be disturbed. Take a few deep breaths to center yourself.
2. **Identify the critic**
   - Close your eyes and take a moment to tune into the voice of your inner critic. Listen to what it says. What phrases or criticisms come up frequently?
   - Open your journal and write down these common phrases or criticisms. Be as specific as possible.
3. **Understand the critic**
   - Reflect on the origins of these criticisms. Ask yourself,
     - *When did I first start hearing these critiques?*
     - *Do these voices remind me of anyone from my past (e.g., parents, teachers, peers)?*
     - *What situations trigger this inner critic the most?*
   - Write your reflections in your journal.
4. **Empathize with the critic**
   - Imagine your inner critic as a separate entity that wants to protect you from failure or harm. Give it a name and visualize it as a character. This helps create a sense of distance and allows you to interact with it more objectively.
   - Write a letter to your inner critic. Start with understanding and empathy. For example:
     - "Dear [Name], I understand that you are trying to protect me by pointing out my flaws. I know you are coming from a place of concern and want to keep me safe. Thank you for your intentions."
5. **Respond with compassion**

- Now, respond to the criticisms with compassion and self-love. For each criticism you wrote earlier, write a compassionate response. For example:
  - Criticism: *You always mess things up.*
  - Response: *I am human, and it's okay to make mistakes. I am learning and growing from each experience.*

6. **Transform the critic**
- Visualize transforming your inner critic into a supportive coach or friend. What would this supportive voice say instead? Rewrite the criticisms as encouraging statements. For example:
  - Criticism: *You're not good enough.*
  - Supportive Statement: *You are capable and worthy just as you are. Keep trying, and you will succeed.*

7. **Create affirmations**
- Turn the supportive statements into positive affirmations. Write these affirmations in your journal and repeat them to yourself daily. For example:
  - *I am worthy and capable.*
  - *I learn and grow from my experiences.*

8. **Practice regularly**
- Set aside time each week to check in with your inner critic. Notice any new criticisms and transform them using the steps above.
- Over time, this practice will help you build a more loving and supportive relationship with yourself.

Reflection

After completing the exercise, take a few moments to reflect on how you feel. Write down any changes you notice in your journal. Do you feel more compassionate toward yourself? Do you notice any shifts in how you handle self-criticism?

By consistently practicing this exercise, you can learn to silence the critical voice in your head and replace it with a loving, supportive one. You can do this regularly to practice the habit of silencing the inner critic, or do this exercise whenever you feel as though the inner critic is now in control in your head.

That day, the ladies ended the session by writing letters of apology to themselves, and all I could hear was silence and sniffing. There was some serious group healing that day, as well as wiping a lot of tears. Just being there and witnessing the beautiful journey of these amazing ladies learning day by day how to build a better relationship with themselves is why I do what I do, and it's what keeps me going and giving more and more.

Hugs were shared, connections were made, and a lot of healing took place that day, so truly never underestimate the power of healing together. This journey doesn't have to be lonely, and as the name of the community says, you are not alone!

Chapter 21: Daily Practices for Self-Acceptance

Humans are a combination of so many parts. Some parts we try to hide. This can be due to certain limiting beliefs we have built about ourselves that hold us from being our true authentic self and getting connected to our true THAT. We have talked about what to stop doing and what to start doing when it comes to loving ourselves. In this chapter, I am including some self-acceptance routines that have worked for me and my clients, and then I end the chapter with a visualization you can use to connect you with yourself and to empower the love within you for yourself.

Here are some of the most amazing things that have helped me, and I encourage all my clients to try them out.

Start the habit of journaling

I mentioned this in Part One, but it's so important I want to mention it again. We have grown up in societies that try to silence us rather than empower our voices, so you will find yourself held back (even personally) when it comes to confronting yourself and others, or even just processing what goes on in your head. Journaling is one of the most impactful tools and has supported so many on their journeys. It can be used to process your emotions, to let go of negative emotions about yourself and others, and to just understand yourself when you don't know why you're feeling the way you feel. A lot of people say they are not writers and that they can barely write, but these are the same people who, once they get into the habit of writing, don't stop and you'll find them writing pages and pages. Other people who say they don't write or can't write are the overthinkers, and not writing can be a coping mechanism because they might fear the thoughts that come into their head. What I would encourage them to do is dissociate the thoughts from who they truly are, because you are not your thoughts! You are you who is thinking, and that means you have control on what to take from your thoughts and what to let go of.

SUCCESS STORIES
with Journaling

I've had many clients who were initially resistant to the idea of journaling as part of their journey to reconnect with their THAT—their true self. The thought of delving into their inner world, facing their fears, and admitting things they had buried deep within was daunting for them. It was like asking them to enter a dark cave with no guarantee of what they might find. The fear of what might surface made them hesitate to start, but the transformative power of journaling is something that can't be ignored.

Journaling, when done consistently and with the right approach, can be an incredibly powerful tool for self-discovery and healing. I always start by teaching my clients some basic tactics: Never lift the pen from the paper, avoid judging what you write, and resist the urge to go back and read what you've written. These simple guidelines help remove the pressure and self-censorship that often hinder honest expression. By letting the words flow freely, without worrying about how they sound or what they reveal, clients start to access parts of themselves they didn't even know existed.

At a *You're Not Alone* session, I asked everyone to pair up with someone they didn't know well, stare into each other's eyes for five minutes without speaking a single word, then each write a letter to the other expressing what she feels the other would want to hear at that moment (encouraging words). The women still recall how impactful that exercise was, because not only do they recall the letter they received that spoke to their soul, but also sharing what they thought the others would want to hear, the majority of which was what they wished to hear themselves. That's one of the powers of writing and journaling. That's how change is created. That's how you build yourself up and develop a better relationship with yourself.

Journaling helps individuals connect with their inner thoughts and emotions in a way often not possible through spoken words alone. According to research, expressive writing can lead to significant improvements in mental and physical health. It does this by helping individuals process their experiences and reduce the burden of negative emotions, allowing people to organize their thoughts, gain perspective, and ultimately, find closure on issues that may have been troubling them for years.

Practice visualization for self-acceptance

Before you start this exercise, I would like you to sit somewhere comfortable, quiet with no distractions (turn your phone off, take off your smart watch, close the TV if you have it on, etc.). Make sure the lighting is not strong, and take a couple of breaths before you tap into the visualization. You can start reading the script as it is here (or scan the QR code on the following page to hear the visualization in my voice).

Find a quiet and comfortable place where you can sit or lie down without interruptions. Close your eyes, take a deep breath, and allow yourself to relax. As you breathe in, imagine breathing in peace and calm. And as you breathe out, release any tension or stress.

Imagine you are in a serene, beautiful garden. The sun is shining warmly, and a gentle breeze is blowing. This is your safe space, a place where you can be yourself fully and completely.

In this garden, there is a comfortable bench. As you sit on this bench, you see a path leading toward you. From this path, you see different versions of yourself approaching. Each version represents a part of you—the parts you love, the parts you hide, your strengths, your weaknesses, and the parts that keep you safe.

One by one, each version of you comes and sits on the bench beside you. Greet each one warmly. Acknowledge their presence and their role in your life. Notice how each part of you feels, looks, and what they represent.

Begin a conversation with these parts of yourself.

To the part you show to the world: Thank you for helping me navigate through life. I appreciate your strength and presence.

To the part you hide: I see you and acknowledge your feelings. You are safe here with me.

To your strengths: Thank you for empowering me and helping me achieve my goals. I am proud of you.

To your weaknesses: I accept you as a part of me. You remind me that it's okay to be human and imperfect.

To the part that keeps you safe: Thank you for protecting me. I value your vigilance and care.

Visualize your true leader, your inner guide, stepping forward. This part of you is wise, compassionate, and confident. Embrace this inner leader and let them guide you in accepting all parts of yourself.

Now, visualize all these parts of yourself coming together in a circle, holding hands. Feel a sense of unity and wholeness. You are a complete being, with all these parts contributing to who you are.

Repeat the following affirmations silently or aloud.
- *I accept all parts of myself.*
- *I am whole and complete as I am.*
- *I embrace my strengths and my weaknesses.*
- *I am grounded by my inner leader.*
- *I love and accept myself fully and completely.*

Take a few deep breaths. Slowly begin to bring your awareness back to your surroundings. Wiggle your fingers and toes, and when you are ready, gently open your eyes.

The Art of Living With Purpose Is to Focus on What We Can Control

One of the key aspects of practicing self-acceptance and living a life of purpose is to focus on what is within our control and let go of what's not within our control. I have had so many clients thinking they need to control everything around them to be able to reach their goals and live a purposeful life. But they tend to forget that they have the power and control over what affects them and what doesn't.

The following table illustrates the distinction between things we can control and things we cannot control. Understanding and accepting these differences is key to maintaining mental and emotional well-being.

Things we can control	Things we cannot control
Our thoughts	Other people's actions
Our actions	Other people's opinions
Our reactions	The past
Our attitude	The future
Our efforts	External events
Our habits	Natural occurrences

Things We Can Control

Our thoughts
- **Mindfulness and positivity** Focus on maintaining a positive mindset and practicing mindfulness to stay present. Don't forget that you have the remote control and button on what to feed into your mind.

Our actions
- **Intentional behavior** Choose actions that align with your values and goals, and act with intention and purpose.

Our reactions
- **Emotional regulation** Work on managing your emotions and responses to various situations, even when they are challenging. Change your perspective on how others are making you feel, and remind yourself that the signals and triggers of how others make you feel truly starts from you. Regulating your emotions helps you regain control.

Our attitude
- **Optimism and resilience** Cultivate a positive and resilient attitude toward life's ups and downs. Build that resilience mindset while still allowing yourself to be a human.

Our effort
- **Consistent effort** Dedicate consistent effort to your tasks and goals, knowing that your input can directly affect the outcome. You are leading your life, and the more effort you put toward YOU, the faster you will see the results.

Our habits
- **Healthy routines** Develop and maintain habits that support your well-being and personal growth. The *Atomic Habits* book has been a game changer for me. James Clear simplified the concept that a 1 percent change in your day-to-day life builds long-lasting habits.

Things We Cannot Control

Other people's actions
- **Acceptance** Accept that you cannot control how others behave. Focus on your own responses and actions. Once you let go of that thought, you are closer to your THAT than you can imagine.

Other people's opinions
- **Self-worth** Recognize that other people's opinions do not define your self-worth. Trust in your own values and beliefs.

Remember that people's opinions reflect their own perception in life and don't reflect you in any way.

The past
- **Letting go** Acknowledge the past, learn from it, and let go of any regrets or resentments. Women tend to ruminate in the past and get stuck there, as if the best days of our lives are in the past, but the truth is there are so many best days you haven't lived yet, so many people you haven't loved yet, and so many goals you haven't accomplished yet. Keep being in the present and working on a better tomorrow.

The future
- **Preparation, not prediction** Although you can prepare for the future, you cannot predict it. Focus on the present and what you can do now. The present is the only "present" you have. Use it wisely. Think about what you can do today that will enhance your tomorrow. And stop overthinking what may or may not happen. When I find myself thinking, *What if it doesn't work out?* I love to remind myself to replace it with *But what if it did?*

External events
- **Adaptability** Understand that external events, such as economic changes or natural disasters, are beyond your control. Adapt and respond as best as you can. We hear a lot about the Agile approach in organizations. It's now time to live that Agile approach in your everyday life. When external events happen, learn how you can pivot and restructure your actions based on that.

Natural occurrences
- **Acceptance** Accept natural occurrences, such as weather or natural disasters, as part of life. Prepare and respond appropriately but recognize their unpredictability.

How to Let Go of Thinking About Things We Cannot Control

Practice mindfulness. Engage in mindfulness activities such as meditation, deep breathing, or yoga to stay present and reduce anxiety about uncontrollable events.

Focus on what you can do. Direct your energy toward actions and thoughts within your control. Set achievable goals and take small steps toward them.

Reframe your thoughts. When you catch yourself worrying about things you can't control, consciously reframe your thoughts to focus on what you can influence.

Accept and let go. Practice acceptance by acknowledging that some things are beyond your control. Let go of the need to control everything and trust in your ability to handle whatever comes your way.

Seek support. Talk to friends, family, or a therapist about your concerns. Sometimes, sharing your worries can help you gain perspective and find ways to cope.

By focusing on what we can control and letting go of what we cannot, we can lead more balanced, peaceful, and fulfilling lives. Our way to our THAT really relies heavily on how we act toward ourselves and what happens around us.

Steps to Letting Go of Shame

Shame is a powerful emotion that can deeply impact our sense of self-worth, our relationships, and our ability to grow. It often lurks in the shadows of our mind, influencing our behavior and limiting our potential without us even realizing it. Overcoming shame is crucial for personal growth, as it allows us to step into our true selves, free from the burdens of past mistakes, societal expectations, and self-judgment.

In this section, we'll explore practical steps to address and overcome shame, along with exercises that promote vulnerability, self-compassion, and ultimately, healing.

Understanding Shame and Its Impact

Before diving into the exercises, it's important to understand the impact of shame. Shame is more than just feeling embarrassed, it's a deep-seated belief that there is something inherently wrong with us. This belief can lead to self-isolation, hinder our personal growth, and create barriers in our relationships.

Shame often manifests in these ways:
- **Self-criticism**: constantly judging oneself harshly and feeling unworthy of love or success
- **Isolation**: withdrawing from others to avoid judgment or rejection
- **Perfectionism**: striving for flawlessness as a way to counteract feelings of inadequacy

- **Fear of vulnerability:** avoiding situations where one might be exposed or judged

The key to overcoming shame is to confront it directly and replace it with healthier, more compassionate ways of thinking and being.

Exercises to Overcome Shame

Vulnerability Exercise: Sharing Your Story

Shame thrives in secrecy. One of the most effective ways to combat shame is through vulnerability—opening up and sharing your experiences with someone you trust.

Exercise

1. **Identify a safe person** Think of someone in your life who you trust and who will listen without judgment. This could be a close friend, a family member, coach or therapist.
2. **Share your story** Begin by sharing a small part of your story that you feel comfortable revealing. This could be something you've been carrying with you, a mistake you've made, or an experience that made you feel ashamed.
3. **Reflect on the experience** After sharing, reflect on how it felt to open up. Notice any feelings of relief, connection, or understanding. Vulnerability can be incredibly freeing and can diminish the power that shame holds over you.

Self-Compassion Practice: Speaking Kindly to Yourself

Shame often leads to harsh self-criticism. Self-compassion is the antidote—it involves treating yourself with the same kindness and understanding that you would offer a friend.

Exercise

1. **Identify negative self-talk** Throughout the day, pay attention to the way you speak to yourself, especially when you make a mistake or feel insecure.
2. **Challenge the critic** When you notice negative self-talk, pause and ask yourself, *Would I say this to someone I care about?* If the answer is no, reframe the thought in a more compassionate way.
3. **Practice daily affirmations** Start each day by looking in the mirror and repeating positive affirmations such as, "I am worthy of love and respect," or "I accept myself as I am, flaws and all." Over time, these affirmations can help rewire your thinking and reduce feelings of shame.

Journaling Exercise: Releasing Shame

Writing is a powerful tool for processing emotions. Journaling allows you to express your feelings in a safe, private space and can help you gain clarity and perspective.

Exercise

1. **Daily reflection** Set aside time each day to journal about your feelings of shame. Write freely, without judgment, about what triggers these feelings and how they affect your life.
2. **Forgiveness letter** Write a letter of forgiveness to yourself. Acknowledge any mistakes or regrets you have and then

offer yourself forgiveness. This exercise can help release the burden of shame and promote healing.
3. **Gratitude journaling** End each journaling session by writing down three things you're grateful for. Focusing on gratitude can shift your mindset from one of shame to one of appreciation and positivity.

The Impact of Shame on Personal Growth and Relationships

Shame can severely impact your ability to grow and thrive. It keeps you stuck in a cycle of self-doubt and fear, preventing you taking risks and pursuing your goals. In relationships, shame can create distance and distrust, as it makes you reluctant to open up or be vulnerable with others.

However, when you begin to address and overcome shame, you open the door to personal growth. You become more willing to take on new challenges, to be honest with yourself and others, and to build deeper, more meaningful connections.

Personal Growth

- **Overcoming limiting beliefs** Shame often manifests as limiting beliefs—ideas about what you can or cannot do. By confronting and letting go of shame, you can start to challenge these beliefs and expand your possibilities.
- **Building resilience** As you work through shame, you build emotional resilience. This resilience allows you to bounce back from setbacks more quickly and to approach life's challenges with a stronger, more confident mindset.

Relationships
- **Enhancing authenticity** Letting go of shame enables you to be more authentic in your relationships. When you're not hiding parts of yourself, you can connect with others on a deeper, more genuine level.
- **Strengthening connections** Vulnerability is the foundation of strong relationships. By being open and honest about your experiences, you invite others to do the same, which can lead to stronger, more trusting connections.

Overcoming shame is not a process that happens overnight, but it is a journey worth taking. By practicing vulnerability, self-compassion, and regular reflection, you can begin to release the grip that shame has on your life. As you do, you'll find that you're more capable of personal growth, stronger in your relationships, and more at peace with who you are.

Remember, shame is not a reflection of your true worth. You are more than your past mistakes, your perceived flaws, or the judgments of others. Embrace the process of letting go of shame and stepping into the fullness of your true self—confident, compassionate, and free.

Recap of Key Messages

This book is a journey back to yourself, a journey of finding your voice, embracing your purpose, and stepping into your power. Each chapter unfolds a new layer, guiding you through the steps to reconnect with the truest, most authentic version of who you are. Here are the core messages from each part of this transformative journey.

- **Know your "why."** Purpose isn't a destination, it's the compass that guides every decision, action, and relationship. Your "why" is what brings meaning to your life, anchoring you in values that help you navigate both joy and adversity. Without it, we drift; with it, we thrive. In knowing your purpose, you create a foundation of strength and clarity that fuels every chapter of your story.
- **Embrace gentle courage.** True courage isn't loud or forceful. It's the quiet strength that comes from showing up authentically, even when doing so feels vulnerable. This courage allows you to face life's challenges with grace and resilience, inspiring you to lead your life with gentleness and conviction. It's not about fearlessness but about moving forward despite it.

- **Build a supportive network.** Surround yourself with people who uplift, inspire, and empower you. A strong support network offers more than companionship. It provides the safety, encouragement, and wisdom needed to grow. Through these connections, you create a foundation of resilience that helps you rise even in the face of challenges.
- **Live with intention and fun.** Life's beauty lies not only in reaching goals but also in the moments of joy, spontaneity, and laughter along the way. Prioritize time for things that light you up, for the simple joys that bring balance and refresh your spirit. When you live intentionally, even the smallest moments feel significant, and your journey becomes not only purposeful but also joyful.
- **Redefine success and embrace failures.** Success is about progress, not perfection. This book explores how each setback is a steppingstone, a powerful opportunity to learn and grow. Failure is not an endpoint but the beginning of a new chapter, a reminder that you're still learning, evolving, and moving forward.
- **Break free from comparison.** Comparison is a thief of joy and a barrier to personal growth. In a world that constantly pressures us to measure up, this book reminds you to honor your unique journey. Embrace your own path, free from the expectations of others, and find liberation in knowing that your worth isn't defined by comparison—it's inherent.
- **Balance stability with passion.** Stability and passion are two sides of the same coin. While passion fuels your drive, stability anchors you, providing the balance

needed to pursue your dreams sustainably. This book shows you how to create harmony between these forces, making space for both structure and spontaneity in your life.
- **Reconnect with yourself.** Amidst the demands of life, reconnecting with your inner self becomes essential. This book provides tools to ground yourself, to listen deeply, and to return to the heart of who you are. This journey of self-reconnection builds self-trust, fostering a relationship with yourself that's resilient, compassionate, and unwavering.
- **Celebrate your growth.** Every step forward, every challenge overcome, is a moment worth celebrating. This book encourages you to acknowledge the small victories as much as the big ones. In celebrating your growth, you honor your journey, recognizing that every experience, every lesson, has contributed to the person you're becoming.
- **Set boundaries with love.** Boundaries are for creating space for what truly matters, not shutting people out. This book guides you in setting boundaries with kindness and clarity, protecting your energy so you can give your best to what matters most. Boundaries, set with love, are essential for a balanced and fulfilling life.
- **Empower your mindset.** Your thoughts shape your reality. This book dives into the power of mindset, showing you how to cultivate positivity, resilience, and self-belief. Through mindset shifts, you unlock the ability to not just cope with life's challenges but to rise above them with strength and grace.

- **Embrace stillness and self-care:** Stillness is where clarity and peace reside. Self-care is about restoration. In a world that glorifies busyness, this book invites you to slow down, to embrace moments of quiet, and to give yourself the gift of rest and reflection. In this stillness, you find the space to reconnect, recharge, and realign.
- **Turn dreams into action.** Dreams become reality through consistent, intentional action. This book provides a framework for transforming aspirations into achievable goals, guiding you in taking deliberate steps that bring you closer to your vision. It's about moving from desire to decision, from inspiration to implementation.
- **Nurture your inner leader.** Leadership begins within. This book explores the power of self-leadership, empowering you to take responsibility for your choices, your growth, and your happiness. In nurturing the leader within, you build a foundation of strength and integrity that impacts not only your life but also the lives of those around you.
- **Stay connected to your values.** Values are the heartbeat of who you are. When you live in alignment with your values, every choice, every action becomes an expression of your truth. This book shows you how to identify and stay true to these values, creating a life that feels authentic, balanced, and deeply meaningful.

This journey is about rediscovering who you are, reclaiming the parts of you that may have been quieted by life's demands, and embracing the wholeness that comes from living with intention. May these lessons, reflections, and practices be a compass as you navigate the path back to yourself, celebrating each step and every moment of growth along the way. Remember, this is not just a book but a guide to creating a life that feels deeply and authentically yours.

You're Not Alone
Community

You're Not Alone is a safe and empowering space for women of all backgrounds, life stages, and aspirations. It's a community where experiences are shared, support is offered, and where each member is encouraged to grow into the truest version of herself. Whether you're navigating a life transition, seeking clarity in your career, or simply looking for a place to share your dreams, this community provides a foundation of support and understanding that feels like a family.

Every woman in the *You're Not Alone* community has her own story, her own struggles, and her own dreams, yet all are united by a shared purpose: to support each other's journeys toward self-discovery and fulfillment. Here, you won't find judgment or expectations. Instead, you'll discover a culture of acceptance, guidance, and friendship, where each member is respected for her unique perspective and strengths.

Why Join the You're Not Alone **Community?**
Imagine having a place to go when you're feeling unsure or overwhelmed, where others understand your journey because they, too, are walking a similar path. Here's what makes *You're Not Alone* a powerful and invaluable community for women everywhere:

- **Authentic connection** In this community, you'll find a sisterhood of women who genuinely care about your well-being. Each connection you make is an opportunity to build a lasting friendship, filled with empathy, understanding, and encouragement.
- **Empowerment through shared experiences** The power of shared stories can be transformational. When women come together to share their challenges, triumphs, and lessons learned, we create a ripple effect of empowerment. Each story becomes a source of inspiration for someone else, proving that although our journeys may be different, our struggles and triumphs often echo one another.
- **Safe space for growth and healing** *You're Not Alone* is built on a foundation of respect and confidentiality. Members can share openly without fear of judgment, creating a safe space for healing and personal growth. Here, vulnerability is seen as strength, and every woman is encouraged to show up as her authentic self.
- **Practical tools for self-development** Members gain access to curated resources, workshops, and discussions led by experienced life coaches, mentors, and professionals who offer actionable tools and insights to help you navigate life's challenges. From confidence-building exercises to goal-setting workshops, every resource is designed to help you grow.
- **Personal and professional support** Whether you're seeking career advice, looking to enhance your leadership skills, or simply need support in a personal matter, *You're Not Alone* offers a wealth of resources tailored to both personal and professional development. It's a place to explore new

ideas, set meaningful goals, and hold yourself accountable with the support of your peers.

How to Join You're Not Alone

Becoming a part of *You're Not Alone* is simple, and it can change your life. Here's how you can join and begin your journey with us.

1. **Visit our website or social media.** Head over to our official website www.coachasmaaa.com/yna-community or follow us on social media to get an initial feel of the community (Instagram: @yna_community). There, you'll find more information about our values, our story, and the women who make up our vibrant community.
2. **Sign up and introduce yourself.** Once you decide to join, sign up on the community platform, where you'll be asked to create a brief introduction about yourself. This helps us connect you with women who share similar goals or interests, making your journey with us meaningful from day one.
3. **Engage in weekly events and discussions.** The community hosts regular events, workshops, and discussion circles designed to deepen connections and provide practical insights for personal growth. Whether it's a virtual meetup or an in-depth workshop, there's always something happening, and every member is encouraged to participate.
4. **Access resources and personalized support.** As a member, you'll have exclusive access to coaching sessions, expert talks, and interactive resources designed to support your growth. You can also choose to connect with a personal mentor, who will be there to guide you through challenges and celebrate your victories.

5. **Give and receive support.** *You're Not Alone* thrives on reciprocal relationships. Here, you're invited to not only receive support but also to share your wisdom, experiences, and encouragement with others. It's a place where everyone's voice matters, and your story can make a difference in someone else's life.

The Value of Joining *You're Not Alone*

When you join *You're Not Alone*, you're joining a community that stands as a testament to the power of togetherness and shared experiences. It's a place that reminds you that you are enough and that your dreams, struggles, and goals are valid. Here, you'll find women who are ready to lift you up, inspire you to grow, and celebrate your every step.

By becoming a member, you're investing in a support system that empowers you to rise above challenges, to reconnect with yourself, and to live a life that reflects your truest values. In this community, every woman is a pillar of strength, and together, we are stronger.

Join Us and Discover the Power of Connection

If you're ready to embrace a journey of growth, connection, and empowerment, then *You're Not Alone* is here for you. Join us, bring your authentic self, and step into a community where you're never truly alone. Whether you're here to learn, share, heal, or grow, *You're Not Alone* will be here to walk alongside you, every step of the way.

Acknowledgments

Writing *Back to THAT* has been a deeply personal journey, and I'm incredibly grateful to the many people who supported me, inspired me, and walked alongside me as this book took shape. This book is for every woman who has felt disconnected, every woman searching for herself, and everyone who has ever struggled to find their way back to who they truly are. It is a tribute to resilience, self-love, and the power of reconnecting with our truest selves. I couldn't have done it alone, and for that, I want to share my heartfelt thanks.

To my family, whose unconditional love and support have been my greatest anchor—thank you. Your belief in me has always been the foundation upon which I build. To my parents, for instilling in me the values of courage, integrity, and kindness; and to my siblings, who have taught me the beauty of connection and the importance of supporting one another through life's journeys.

To my friends, thank you for reminding me to stay grounded and true to myself, even when the journey was challenging. Your words of encouragement, countless cups of coffee, and endless laughter made every moment of writing this book feel lighter and more joyous.

To my community, *You're Not Alone*, this book is as much yours as it is mine. Your stories, struggles, and triumphs were my constant source of inspiration. Watching each of you grow, reclaim yourselves, and redefine your journeys has been my greatest honor. Thank you for trusting me to guide you, and for reminding me daily why I do what I do.

To my mentors and coaches, who have been my guiding lights, thank you for helping me find clarity, confidence, and purpose. Your insights, encouragement, and wisdom gave me the courage to turn my vision into a reality, and your presence in my life has been transformative.

A special thank you to my team, whose dedication brought this book to life in ways I could have never imagined. To my editor, who guided me with a thoughtful and gentle hand, helping me find my voice with every draft, and to my publishing team, for believing in my message and helping me share it with the world. Thank you for turning my words into something I am proud to call mine.

Lastly, to the readers of *Back to THAT*, thank you. Thank you for choosing to spend time within these pages, for trusting me to walk alongside you on your journey back to yourself. This book reflects the hope, strength, and courage that I believe resides in all of us. My hope is that as you read, you find your own path to self-love, self-discovery, and purpose. Remember, this journey is one we walk together, and you are never alone.

With love and gratitude,
Asmaa

About the Author

Asmaa Alkuwari is a trailblazer in life and executive coaching, a TEDx speaker, and a dedicated advocate for women's empowerment, whose voice and vision have inspired audiences both locally and internationally. Known for her pioneering role as the first Qatari woman and the youngest to lead the International Coaching Federation Chapter in Doha, Asmaa has set new standards in the coaching profession within Qatar and beyond, using her influence to elevate the field and create a lasting impact.

With over five years of coaching and training experience and twelve years in the corporate world, Asmaa has worked with hundreds of clients, guiding them toward greater confidence, resilience, and purpose in both their personal and professional lives. Her unique approach to coaching combines her expertise in user experience (UX) with her passion for empowering women to lead authentically, establishing her as one of the most influential figures in executive coaching in the region.

In 2019, Asmaa founded *You're Not Alone*, a community dedicated to creating a safe, supportive, and empowering space for women. Since its inception, the community has hosted more than eighty diverse events, drawing over 2,500 women in cumulative attendance. Today, *You're Not Alone* has over 150 active members, all benefiting from an environment where they can connect, share, and grow. Her dedication to community work earned her the Silver Prize for Women Changing the World MENA Award in the category of Community Impact; the winner of "Change Catalyst" for Playbook Awards, recognizing her significant contributions to creating lasting social change; and silver winner of "Life Coach of the Year" for the Coaching Awards 2024.

As an ICF-certified coach (PCC), motivational speaker, and trusted mentor, Asmaa has collaborated with prestigious organizations in delivering tailored training programs to their leaders. She is also a frequent guest on both local and international podcasts, where she shares her insights on leadership, self-empowerment, and UX-driven coaching with a broader audience. Her thought-provoking articles on LinkedIn provide fresh perspectives for leaders striving to create meaningful change within their teams and themselves.

Her latest work, *Back to THAT*, is a heartfelt guide dedicated to helping women reconnect with their truest selves. Alongside her book, Asmaa's upcoming wellness stationery brand and numerous community initiatives continue her mission to provide practical tools and spaces for personal and professional growth.

Asmaa's work, voice, and vision are all devoted to encouraging women on their journeys of self-discovery and empowerment. Through *Back to THAT*, *You're Not Alone,* and her impactful coaching and community initiatives, Asmaa remains unwavering in her mission to inspire, uplift, and help others redefine their lives on their own terms.

About the Publisher

The Dreamwork Collective is a print and digital publisher sharing diverse voices and powerful stories with the world. Dedicated to the advancement of humanity, we strive to create books that have a positive impact on people and on the planet. Our hope is that our books document this moment in time for future generations to enjoy and learn from, and that we play our part in ushering humanity into a new era of heightened creativity, connection, and compassion.

www.thedreamworkcollective.com
[O] thedreamworkcollective

www.ingramcontent.com/pod-product-compliance
Lightning Source LLC
LaVergne TN
LVHW041929070526
838199LV00051BA/2758